7 KEYS
To Unlock
Your Full Potential

D0168290

www.7keystounlock.com

WHAT OTHERS SAY ABOUT THIS BOOK

"I have seldom read a book that so clearly leaves the reader to better understand the incredible relationship between the conscious and subconscious areas of the mind. I highly recommend it."
> —Jack Canfield, Co-author of the *Chicken Soup for the Soul* series
> and a featured teacher in "The Secret."

"This book has the power and capacity to totally change your life! I guarantee it."
> —George Zimmer, Executive Chairman, Men's Wearhouse, retired

"Sometimes a book comes along that offers the reader a life changing opportunity. Murphy and Jensen have written one that does just that. I know from first hand experience how you can improve your life by putting to work the principles and concepts contained in *7 KEYS To Unlock Your Full Potential*. If you are going to read one book this year, make it this one."
> —Howard Behar, President, Starbucks Coffee International, retired

"The root cause of human suffering is often thought to lie outside us. And yet, as Murphy and Jensen point out, it really lies within our subconscious mind. So too, we are so clearly reminded, lies the source of great joy and possibility. This book is essential reading for anyone who wants to wake up to their fullest capacities. As the authors note, consciousness 'brings guidance, freedom, and peace of mind.' The adventure of our unfolding potentials awaits us all."
> —Marilyn Mandala Schlitz, Ph.D., Former President/CEO,
> Institute of Noetic Sciences.

"There is a musical form termed "call and response" in which a distinct phrase is played by one musician and a second phrase forms a commentary on or a response to the first phrase. This mirrors a tradition characteristic of African and African American Christian worship in which the speaker makes a statement and the congregation responds with an affirmation, amplifying and clarifying the initial statement. This work by Murphy and Jensen is an exquisite example of call and response—Murphy asserts, Jensen elucidates. Their subject matter may have sometimes been dismissed as too far out or not based on verifiable scientific evidence, but in page after page the call is a clear, declaratory statement of conviction and the response is an offering of anecdotal evidence which becomes increasingly compelling as the chapters accumulate. If it is not enough to convince the skeptic, it is at least enough to shake the certainty and smugness of its critics. Read this and sing!"
> —Daniel K. Church, Ph.D., President, Bastyr University.

"We all grew up with the saying, "Seeing is believing." Only after reading Jim Jensen's book did I appreciate that "believing leads to seeing." The power and goodness of the Universe lies within each of us. This book gives us the key to access and focus that power to make our hopes and beliefs a reality. The universal wisdom in its chapters has changed my life forever. . . . as it will for anyone who reads it."

—Doug Jewett, CEO, Ramgen Power Systems, Inc.

"Every paragraph of *7 KEYS To Unlock Your Full Potential* is filled with wisdom and keen insight. I've seen thousands of people who became over-whelmed by outside forces and who felt powerless as a result. Jim Jensen has brilliantly illuminated the sources of power, healing and growth that lie dormant inside each of us. Everyone will benefit from reading this fine book and taking its profound lessons to heart. You'll be astonished at the power that lies right at your fingertips."

—John P. Rochon, Former Chairman and
CEO of Mary Kay Cosmetics, Inc.

"Drawing upon knowledge from both the wisdom traditions and contemporary research, *7 KEYS To Unlock Your Full Potential* shows us ways to advance the exploration of our soul's further reaches. Every one of us can participate in this adventure, on the greatest of all human frontiers."

—Michael Murphy, Founder of the Esalen Institute and
author of *The Future of the Body.*

"The greatest frontier is not the skies or the ocean. It is understanding the power of our miraculous selves. Herein is the primer to get started. Jensen's book is perfect for the action oriented 21st century. The central themes of Dr Murphy's landmark work set the stage. Excerpts from many of the finest thinkers of the last generation clarify and reinforce the salient points. Then the closer: Jim's specific steps of how to implement the most powerful prin-ciples of anyone's life. Get ready to be energized!"

—Stan Freimuth, Retired Chairman & CEO, Ragen MacKenzie, Inc.

"This book is uniquely written and formatted in such a way that one could read this once and begin to take charge of one's life in ways to manifest unbe-lievable positive improvements. May I suggest starting with the last chapter on Enlightenment and then reading it cover to cover. I know it will enhance your life as it already has mine

—Lyle Anderson, Chairman, The Lyle Anderson Companies, LLC.

7 KEYS
To Unlock
Your Full Potential

by
C. James Jensen

With Foreword and Contributions by
Lee Pulos, Ph.D., ABPP

www.7keystounlock.com

A Waterside Publication

Published by Waterside Publications
ISBN: 978-1-937504-95-3
WP139P

Manufactured in the United States of America or in Great Britain, when purchased
outside of North or South America

Produced and distributed for
Waterside Publications by
Worthy Shorts Publisher Services BackOffice
A CustomWorthy edition

For further information contact
info@worthyshorts.com

*Man alone, of all the creatures on
Earth, can change his own pattern.
Man alone is architect of his destiny.
The greatest revolution in our
generation is the discovery that human
beings, by changing the inner attitudes
of their minds, can change the outer
aspects of their lives.*

William James

Dedication

This book is dedicated to my grandchildren, Maya, Tucker and Cole, and to all the children of planet Earth. The future of our civilization rests in your hands. Only through the evolution of the consciousness of the human species can we fully live in a world of peace, love and harmony. Just as slavery became a no longer acceptable alternative in the United States in the mid 1800s, our future generations need to abolish the notion that it is acceptable to take another person's life because of differences in religious, political, or any other ideologies or beliefs.

We collectively, do create our own reality.

Bompa

Contents

KEY Number 5: AFFIRMATIONS AND VISUALIZATION
Understanding the power in developing mastery in the proper use of Affirmations and Affirmation Techniques.

KEY Number 6: CREATIVE PROBLEM SOLVING
Understanding the miraculous power of your Supraconscious, the third area of the mind.

**KEY Number 7 RELEASE YOUR FULL
    POTENTIAL**
**Understanding who we REALLY are and the need to
dispose of our "Mental Garbage" on a daily basis.**

Introduction

by C. James Jensen

Dr. Joseph Murphy was an early pioneer in the field of self image psychology. I first became aware of his teachings in 1969 although I had not heard of his name nor was I aware he had written The Power of Your Subconscious Mind in 1963.

In October, 1969, my wife, Jeri, and I attended a four day seminar called Executive Dynamics. It was taught by its founder, the late John Boyle. Later the same seminar was renamed Omega. We were immensely impressed by the content as we had never been exposed to such teachings previously.

What we learned over the four days was the powerful relationship between the conscious and subconscious areas of the mind. We learned how the subconscious is always carrying out the "instructions" given to it by the conscious area of the mind, for better or for worse. We are constantly talking to ourselves ("Self Talk") making assessments of what we like, don't like, what we are "good" at and where we are simply "incompetent". What we will learn throughout this book is how our attitudes, beliefs, opinions and judgments all shape who and what we become. Most people go through life continuing to describe themselves as they have "always been," excelling in some areas and performing poorly in others.

What we learned from John Boyle is that we can personally take charge in changing or re-shaping certain beliefs or thought patterns that no longer serve us well, and there are specific tools we can learn to facilitate such changes. Those tools are taught in this book.

Over the next 40 years, I would not only attend numerous Omega seminars, but I became an impassioned Omega instructor as well. I often asked John where he had learned the content of Omega, and the only answer he gave me was that he had studied with a man named Joseph Murphy. This was before the Internet so there was no way to "Google" Joseph Murphy nor did John tell me Murphy had written a book.

As I gained fluency and understanding of the principles of Omega, I began to look beyond Omega to every book and seminar I could experience to help deepen my understanding of the subconscious and the power of our intentional thoughts. Many roads would eventually lead to one author, Dr. Joseph Murphy.

In 2005, a colleague of mine, Tom Popa, came into my office and handed me a book that he thought I would enjoy. The book was The Power of Your Subconscious Mind by Dr. Joseph Murphy. I thought, "Oh my God! Could this be the same Joseph Murphy that John Boyle had studied with?" In fact, it was.

As I read the book, word by word I realized that the content of the Omega Seminar had come largely from this book, and John Boyle's brilliance was the construction of a four day format that enabled the participants to really "get it" and emerge with a tool kit that enabled them to bring about whatever changes in their lives they desired.

As stated earlier in this introduction, Dr. Joseph Murphy was truly one of "the great early pioneers in the area of self image psychology". Since his book was first written in 1963, there has been so much more added through research to this exciting field of study. Also, the world in which we live today is considerably different than it was over 50 years ago.

My first thoughts were to revise and edit Dr. Murphy's original text and simply add the words "Newly Revised and Edited" following the title, The Power of Your Subconscious Mind. But, as I continued my research and editing, I found more and more contemporary data that truly enabled me to provide the 21st Century edition of Dr. Murphy's original work.

What I have attempted to do in this revised edition of Dr. Murphy's original book is provide the reader with new research and findings in this field. I have also added many "how to" tools that were not included in his original text.

So that the reader can easily distinguish between the text originally written by Dr. Murphy and text added by me, I have used his original serif type for the words written by Dr. Murphy and sans serif for those words written by me.

It is hoped that this revised edition can become a real life-changer for many, as the teachings in the book are not taught in most of our schools or universities.

My deepest appreciation comes from the thousands of individuals, over more than 40 years, who have shared with me their profound transformational experiences; miraculous breakthroughs in personal health, relation-

ships, parenting, teaching, business, and much more. These testimonials followed a pattern of using several or all of the seven key principles written in this book, thus the title, 7 KEYS to Unlock Your Full Potential. These seven keys are highlighted in the Table of Contents.

As is written in Jane Roberts brilliant book, Seth Speaks*:

"Many people, I hear, have lived within New York City and never taken a tour through the Empire State Building, while many foreigners are well acquainted with it. And so while you have a physical address, I may still be able to point out some very strange and miraculous psychic and psychological structures within your own system of reality that you have ignored.

I hope, quite frankly, to do far more than this. I hope to take you on a tour through the levels of reality that are available to you, and to guide you on a journey through the dimensions of your own psychological structure—to open up whole areas of your own consciousness of which you have been relatively unaware. I hope, therefore, not only to explain the multidimensional aspects of personality, but to give each reader some glimpse of that greater identity that is his own."

(Highly recommended reading, Seth Speaks, by Jane Roberts.*)

This is also the hope Dr. Murphy and I wish to provide for you in the pages that follow.

_____

*Roberts, Jane. Seth Speaks. Prentice Hall, 1972

Foreword

By Lee Pulos, Ph.D., ABPP

It is indeed an honor to be invited to write the Forward to *7 KEYS To Unlock Your Full Potential,* a book based on Dr. Joseph Murphy's work, *The Power of Your Subconscious Mind*, which I read over forty years ago and can still remember the visionary and psychological excitement I experienced at that time.

(This is not the same book I first read, however, as Jim Jensen has judiciously and wisely edited and reframed some of the concepts that were valid in 1963 and has redefined and upgraded them so they are consistent with current neuroscience, psychological theory and research.)

The essence of Dr. Murphy's book has not changed. Our ego or conscious mind skims just the top most surface of reality and awareness and focuses on the limited confines of our five senses. However, the unrecognized and heroic portions of our psyche lie beneath the prosaic life.

Unfortunately, most scientists today believe that mind somehow emerges from a mysterious but unprovable interaction of molecules in the brain; thus, matter creates mind. This leads to a very reductionistic and limiting explanation of who we are—a cosmic pessimism of human potential and our deeper beingness.

However, Joseph Murphy's brilliant insights about the depth and richness of our different thresholds of intelligence and corridors of consciousness has helped millions of men and women discover what we have known in the deepest regions of our hearts and minds—but have forgotten that we know it. That is, we are much, much more than our rational minds.

7 KEYS To Unlock Your Full Potential is a reminder of some of the oldest wisdom such as that of the Buddha who said, "A man is the product of his thoughts." And from an even older tradition, the *Bhagavad Gita*, "Man is made by his belief—as he believes, so he is."

The rational mind can be a barrier to the full use of our potential. It limits our capabilities with such a tight focus and has philosophically cut us off from the experimental theatre of our subconscious, the true source of our power. The older-growth forests of the mind contain the true potential—our intuition, our non-ordinary awareness, our dreams, our connection to the cosmic information field, our psychological and spiritual landscapes, and, yes, our mysticism.

This is a book for every generation, in that it comes closest to suggesting an evolutionary adventure that can be comprehended and utilized by every age ranging from a twelve-year-old to his or her grandparents. It also follows and embraces one of Einstein's favorite sayings, "Make everything as simple as possible—but not simpler."

In reading *7 KEYS To Unlock Your Full Potential*, I experienced a great joy in following the bold sweep of Joseph Murphy's and Jim Jensen's thoughts which ranged from the potential for creating miracles, how to awaken our deeper mind for physical and mental healing, overcoming limiting beliefs and fear-driven behavior, developing an inner sense for deserving wealth consciousness, creating healing dreams, overcoming roadblocks to success and how to re-educate and re-program our subconscious for attaining goals and creating and stepping into the most optimal, loving, successful, healthy future possible. And yes, there is even more.

But what resonated most for me throughout the book was how our life is a printout of our beliefs. We create what we focus or concentrate on, and our beliefs are largely responsible for the areas in which we focus most attention. Our life experiences then will follow our focus, beliefs, expectations and intention. The implications of Murphy's and Jensen's insights are unlimited in that, if we don't deal with our limiting beliefs, they will deal with us, in our health, work, relationships, financial prosperity or other areas of our life. Most important, however, Jensen provides the tools and techniques to overcome the psychological antibodies we sometimes set up against ourselves that can impede change.

However, at the very root of every success or failure is self-esteem. It is the official and most important headquarters or base of operations that determines what kind of experiences we attract into our lives. It is the hub of the wheel of life which contains and holds together all the spokes that are necessary for creating and living our dreams easily, effortlessly, without struggle.

Of the thousands of patients I have seen over the years for a variety of issues, I would estimate that at least 95 percent of them had an issue with self-esteem, a sense of worthiness or unworthiness, which can influence the inner sense of deserving love, success, health or prosperity.

To keep it simple, however, this book has described in various ways the three most important tools for manifestation, or giving vocal cords to the subconscious.

Desire is the first tool for creating change. All change begins with desire, which is the purest of potential seeking manifestation or change. It is the fire in the belly of the beast. Even Plato recognized the importance of desire, which in his words, "Must drive the soul with a reigned-in craziness."

The second tool is *expectation*, which follows desire. Expectation awakens our slumbering giant, the subconscious, which then leads to our behavior becoming a self-fulfilling prophecy. Expectation is at the root of, and responsible for, all placebo responses in double blind studies. Lowering your expectations, of course, ensures you won't succeed.

The third tool of manifestation is *imagination*, creating the visualizations and mental movies of the successful future you wish to attain. Imagination breathes life into your goals and is the mental energy for creating your most optimal and brilliant future.

This book is a complete mental tool box that has taken the wisdom of the ages and legitimized it into a vocabulary that we can easily understand and embrace; how to release the past and become more than we ever thought possible. More important, it connects us with the heroic of our strong inner self, the magic within that is yearning to find expression.

Lee Pulos, Ph.D., ABPP
Clinical Psychologist
Author, *The Biology of Empowerment,*
and *The Power of Visualization*

7 KEYS
To Unlock
Your Full Potential

www.7keystounlock.com

Key 1

TAKE CHARGE

Understanding the TRUE
Relationship Between the
Conscious and Subconscious
Areas of the Mind..

How This Book Can
Work Miracles In Your Life

By Dr. Joseph Murphy

I have seen miracles happen to men and women in all walks of life all over the world. Miracles will happen to you, too—when you begin using the magic power of your subconscious mind. This book is designed to teach you that your habitual thinking and imagery mold, fashion, and create your destiny; for as a man thinketh in his subconscious mind, so is he.

Unique feature of this book

The unique feature of this book is its down-to-earth practicality. Here you are presented with simple, usable techniques and formulas which you can easily apply in your everyday world. I have taught these simple processes to men and women all over the world, and recently over a thousand men and women attended a special class in Los Angeles where I presented the highlights of what is offered in the pages of this book. The special features of this book will appeal to you because they show you why oftentimes you get the opposite of what you asked for and reveal to you the reasons why. People have asked me in all parts of the world and thousands of times, "Why is it I have prayed and prayed and got no answer?" In this book you will find the reasons for this common complaint. The many ways of impressing the subconscious mind and getting the right answers make this an extraordinarily valuable book and an ever-present help in time of trouble.

There is one mind common to all individual men (Emerson)

The miracle-working powers of your subconscious mind existed before you and I were born. It is with these thoughts in mind that I urge you in the following chapters to lay hold of this wonderful, magical, transforming power which will bind up mental and physical wounds, proclaim liberty to the fear-ridden mind, and liberate you completely from the limitations of poverty, failure, misery, lack, and frustration. All you have to do is unite mentally and emotionally with the good you wish to embody, and the creative powers of your subconscious will respond accordingly. Begin now, today, to let wonders happen in your life!

"All thoughts are prayers, and all prayers are answered"—positive or negative.

*Think about that. All thoughts are prayers and all prayers are answered—positive or negative. A basic operating principle of this book is **any thought held on a continuous basis in the conscious mind must be brought into reality by the subconscious mind.***

*We don't get what we want, we get what we expect, unless what we want and what we expect are the same. We may desperately want our marriage or our business to be successful, for example. But if the internal stream of dialog occurring in our conscious mind is, "My marriage is falling apart," or "My buiness is failing," this is the result we are **commanding** our subconscious mind to fulfill.*

*Dr. Murphy shows us **precisely** why there can be no other result and precisely how becoming fully aware of the cybernetics, or interaction between the conscious and subconscious areas of the mind, is the key to creating the realities we desire and deserve.*

> In life, you often don't get what you want. But . . . here's what you do get—you get what you expect.
> Ultimately, the world treats you more or less the way you expect to be treated.
>
> *The Go-Givers** by Burg & Mann

*Burg, Bob and John David Mann, The Go-Givers. Portfolio Hardcover, 2007

1

The Treasure House Within You

Infinite riches are all around you if you will open your mental eyes and behold the treasure house of infinity within you. There is a gold mine within you from which you can extract everything you need to live life gloriously, joyously, and abundantly.

Many are sound asleep because they do not know about this gold mine of infinite intelligence and boundless love within themselves. Whatever you want, you can draw forth. A magnetized piece of steel will lift about twelve times its own weight, and if you demagnetize this same piece of steel, it will not even lift a feather. Similarly, there are two types of people. There is the magnetized person who if full of confidence and faith. He knows that he is born to win and to succeed. Then, there is the type of person who is demagnetized. He is full of fears and doubts. Opportunities come, and he says, "I might fail; I might lose my money; people will laugh at me." This type of person will not get very far in life because, if he is afraid to go forward, he will simply stay where he is. Become a magnetized person and discover the master secret of the ages.

The master secret of the ages

What, in your opinion, is the master secret of the ages? The secret of atomic energy? The neutron bomb? Interplanetary travel? No—not any of these. Then, what is this master secret? Where can one find it, and how can it be contacted and brought into action? The answer is extraordinarily simple. This secret is the marvelous, miracle-working power found in your own subconscious mind, the last place that most people would seek it.

The marvelous power of your subconscious

You can bring into your life more power, more wealth, more health, more happiness, and more joy by learning to contact and release the hidden power of your subconscious mind.

You need not acquire this power; you already possess it. But you want to learn how to use it; you want to understand it so that you can apply it in all areas of your life.

As you follow the simple techniques and processes set forth in this book, you can gain the necessary knowledge and understanding. You can be inspired by a new light, and you can generate a new force enabling you to realize your hopes and make all your dreams come true. Decide now to make your life grander, greater, richer, and nobler than ever before.

Within your subconscious depths lie infinite wisdom, infinite power, and an infinite supply of all that is necessary, which is waiting for development and expression. Begin now to recognize these potentialities of your deeper mind, and they will take form in the world without.

The infinite intelligence within your subconscious mind can reveal to you everything you need to know at every moment of time and point of space provided you are open-minded and receptive. You can receive new thoughts and ideas enabling you to bring forth new inventions, make new discoveries, or write books and plays. Moreover, the infinite intelligence in your subconscious can impart to you wonderful kinds of knowledge of an original nature. It can reveal to you and open the way for its perfect expression and true place in your life.

Through the wisdom of your subconscious mind you can attract the ideal companion, as well as the right business associate or partner. It can find the right buyer for your home, and provide you with all the money you need, and the financial freedom to be, to do, and to go as your heart desires.

It is your right to discover this inner world of thought, feeling, and power, of light, love, and beauty. Though invisible, its forces are mighty. Within your subconscious mind you will find the solution for every problem, and the cause for every effect. Because you can draw out the hidden powers, you come into actual possession of the power and wisdom necessary to move forward in abundance, security, joy, and dominion.

I have seen the power of the subconscious lift people up out of crippled states, making them whole, vital, and strong once more, and free to go out into the world to experience happiness, health, and joyous expression. There is a miraculous healing power in your subconscious that can heal the troubled mind and the broken heart. It can open the prison door of the mind and liberate you. It can free you from all kinds of material and physical bondage.

Necessity of a working basis

Substantial progress in any field of endeavor is impossible in the absence of a working basis which is universal in its application. You can become skilled in the operation of your subconscious mind. You can practice its powers with a certainty of results in exact proportion to your knowledge of its principles and to your application of them for definite specific purposes and goals you wish to achieve.

Your thoughts are answered because your subconscious mind is principle, and by principle I mean the way a thing works. For example, the principle of electricity is that it works from a higher to a lower potential. You do not change the principle of electricity when you use it, but by co-operating with nature, you can bring forth marvelous inventions and discoveries which bless humanity in countless ways.

All your experiences, events, conditions, and acts are the reactions of your subconscious mind to your thoughts. Remember, it is not the thing believed in, but the belief in your own mind which brings about the result. Cease believing in the false beliefs, opinions, superstitions, and fears of mankind. Begin to believe in the eternal verities and truths of life which never change. Then, you will move onward and upward.

As Bruce H. Lipton, Ph.D., wrote in his remarkable book, Spontaneous Evolution.*

The subconscious mind controls 95 percent of our behavior and gene-regulating cognitive activity through programs obtained primarily from the field of beliefs. When we take command of

*Lipton, Bruce H. and Steve Bhaerman. Spontaneous Evolution: Hay House, 2009

our own subconscious beliefs and emotions, individually and collectively, we take back creative control over our lives.

Whoever reads this book and applies the principles of the subconscious mind herein set forth, will be able to think scientifically and effectively for himself and for others. Your thoughts are answered according to the universal law of action and reaction. Thought is incipient action. The reaction is the response from your subconscious mind which corresponds with the nature of your thought. Busy your mind with the concepts of harmony, health, peace, and good will, and wonders will happen in your life.

The conscious and subconscious minds

An excellent way to get acquainted with the two functions of your mind is to look upon your own mind as a garden. You are a gardener, and you are planting seeds (thoughts) in your subconscious mind all day long, based on your habitual thinking. As you sow in your subconscious mind, so shall you reap in your body and environment.

When your mind thinks correctly, when you understand the truth, when the thoughts deposited in your subconscious mind are constructive, harmonious, and peaceful, the magic working power of your subconscious will respond and bring about harmonious conditions, agreeable surroundings, and the best of everything. When you begin to control your thought process, you can apply the powers of your subconscious to any problem or difficulty. In other words, you will actually be consciously co-operating with the infinite power and omnipotent law which governs all things.

A knowledge of the interaction of your conscious and subconscious minds will enable you to transform your whole life. In order to change external conditions, you must change the cause. Most people try to change conditions and circumstances by working with conditions and circumstances. To remove discord, confusion, lack, and limitation, you must remove the cause, and the cause is the way you are using your conscious mind. In other words, the way you are thinking and picturing in your mind.

It is fascinating and intensely interesting to observe how you can speak authoritatively and with conviction to the irrational movement of your deeper self bringing silence, harmony, and peace to your mind. The subconscious is subject to the conscious mind, and that is why it is called subconscious or subjective.

Outstanding differences and modes of operation

You will perceive the main differences by the following illustrations: The conscious mind is like the navigator or captain at the bridge of a ship. He directs the ship and signals orders to men in the engine room, who in turn control all the boilers, instruments, gauges, etc. The men in the engine room do not know where they are going; they follow orders. They would go on the rocks if the man on the bridge issued faulty or wrong instructions based on his findings with the compass, sextant, or other instruments. The men in the engine room obey him because he is in charge and issues orders which are automatically obeyed. Members of the crew do not talk back to the captain; they simply carry out orders.

The captain is the master of his ship, and his decrees are carried out. Likewise, your conscious mind is the captain and the master of your ship, which represents your body, environment, and all your affairs. Your subconscious mind takes the orders you give it based upon what your conscious mind believes and accepts as true.

Let's examine this more closely. This is a very powerful metaphor. Our conscious mind is like the captain on a ship barking out commands to the crew, or subconscious mind. In this example, the crew (subconscious) is in the hold of the ship below the water line. The crew can't see nor do they care where the ship is going. They simply carry out the orders of the captain not minding whether the ship runs into another ship, hits an iceberg, or gets the ship safely to its final destination. The crew (subconscious) is completely nonjudgmental. It doesn't question the captain (orders from the conscious mind) or make alternative suggestions, it simply carries out the orders (instructions) precisely. Our subconscious is a servo- mechanism (i.e., servant) whose purpose is to be of service to the conscious mind. Therefore, if we constantly tell our self, and others, "I can never

remember names," for example, the subconscious mind responds simi-
larly, and as you are scanning your memory bank to recall a specific name
*you want to remember, your subconscious will **deliberately** block out that*
name so you "can't remember" it, because those are the instructions it
has received repeatedly from the conscious mind, i.e., "I can never re-
member names."

The subconscious is such a powerful tool and as we learn more fully how
to deliberately engage it, we can consciously direct it to serve us consistently
to achieve the quality of life we truly desire.

I remember teaching a seminar years ago and a married couple shared
with the participants how every June all members of their family got a com-
mon cold. This had been a "family tradition" for over 20 years. They shared
how this had become part of their individual and family "self talk" for years.
"I (we) always get a cold in June." And, sure enough, the subconscious car-
ried out its orders and a cold was manifested by all, every year, every family
member. If one didn't want to break this pattern they could simply chalk it up
to their "genes" and keep affirming the intended result. The fun thing about
this story is through the techniques taught in this book, the family changed
the instructions to the subconscious through a revision in their self talk, or
affirmations (see Chapter 8). I received a letter two years later informing me
that this old pattern had been eliminated and all members of the family had
not had a cold in over two years. The family lived in the same house, in the
same city, with the same weather patterns, but with a revised health "pic-
ture" that simply did not allow or include common colds every June ,or any
other month for that matter.

When you repeatedly say to people, "I can't afford it," then your subconscious mind takes you at your word and sees to it that you will not be
in a position to purchase what you want. As long as you persist in saying,
"I can't afford that car, that trip to Europe, that new home, etc.," you can
rest assured that your subconscious mind will follow your orders, and you
will go through life experiencing the lack of all these things.

Another simple illustration is this: When you say, "I do not like
mushrooms," and the occasion subsequently comes that you are served
mushrooms in sauces or salads, you will get indigestion because your
subconscious mind says to you, "The boss (your conscious mind) does
not like mushrooms." This is an amusing example of the outstanding

differences and modes of operation of your conscious and subconscious minds.

A woman may say, "I wake up at three o'clock, if I drink coffee at night." Whenever she drinks coffee, her subconscious mind nudges her, as if to say, "The boss wants you to stay awake tonight."

Your subconscious mind works twenty-four hours a day and makes provisions for your benefit, pouring all the fruit of your habitual thinking into your lap.

Brief summary of ideas worth remembering

1. The treasure house is within you. Look within for the answer to your heart's desire.
2. The great secret possessed by the great people of all ages was their ability to contact and release the powers of their subconscious mind. You can do the same.
3. Your subconscious has the answer to all problems. If you suggest to your subconscious prior to sleep, "I want to get up at 6 a.m.," it will awaken you at that exact time.
4. Your subconscious mind is the builder of your body and can heal you. Lull yourself to sleep every night with the idea of perfect health, and your subconscious , being your faithful servant, will obey you.
5. Every thought is a cause, and every condition is an effect.
6. If you want to write a book, write a wonderful play, give a better talk to your audience, convey the idea lovingly and feelingly to your subconscious mind, and it will respond accordingly.
7. You are like a captain navigating a ship. He must give the right orders, and likewise, you must give the right orders (thoughts and images) to your subconscious mind which controls and governs all your experiences.
8. Never use the terms, "I can't afford it" or "I can't do this." Your subconscious mind takes you at your word and sees to it that you do not have the money or the ability to do what you want to do. Affirm, "I can do all things through the power of my subconscious mind."

9. The law of life is the law of belief. A belief is a thought in your mind. Do not believe in things to harm or hurt you. Believe in the power of your subconscious to heal, inspire, strengthen, and prosper you.
10. Change your thoughts, and you change your destiny.

Let me introduce you to "self talk." Self talk is that little voice in your head that is talking all the time. If you are asking, "What little voice?" that is the one we are talking about. As you are reading these words you are simultaneously talking to yourself. You may be agreeing or disagreeing with what you are reading, you may be thinking about an email you need to respond to, or what you are having for dinner. That little voice asks questions and the same little voice answers the question. It's all rather bizarre and at times it gets quite busy "in there."

*But, it is our conscious mind that is doing all this chattering and it is important to become aware that such chatter is also providing input and instruction to the subconscious. As we become more knowing, more consciously aware that our present thoughts determine our future, we may choose to more carefully monitor the quality of our thoughts and begin to eliminate or change those thoughts that no longer serve us well. The good news is that since we can only focus on one thought at a time, we **can** control our thoughts. As we introduce the concept of affirmations and affirmation techniques, your understanding and appreciation of the power of self talk will expand. Chapter 3 will elaborate more fully on the crucially important subject of "self talk."*

2

How Your Own Mind Works

You have a mind, and you should learn how to use it. There are two levels of your mind—the conscious or rational level, and the subconscious or irrational level. You think with your conscious mind, and whatever you habitually think sinks down into your subconscious mind, which creates according to the nature of your thoughts. Your subconscious mind is the seat of your emotions and is the creative mind. If you think good, good will follow; if you think evil, evil will follow. This is the way your mind works.

The main point to remember is once the subconscious mind accepts an idea, it begins to execute it. It is an interesting and subtle truth that the law of the subconscious mind works for good and bad ideas alike. This law, when applied in a negative way, is the cause of failure, frustration, and unhappiness. However, when your habitual thinking is harmonious and constructive, you experience perfect health, success, and prosperity.

Peace of mind and a healthy body are inevitable when you begin to think and feel in the right way. Whatever you claim mentally and feel as true, your subconscious mind will accept and bring forth into your experience. The only thing necessary for you to do is to get your subconscious mind to accept your idea, and the law of your own subconscious mind will bring forth the health, peace, or the position you desire. You give the command or decree, and your subconscious will faithfully reproduce the idea impressed upon it. The law of your mind is this: You will get a reaction or response from your subconscious mind according to the nature of the thought or idea you hold in your conscious mind.

Psychologists and psychiatrists point out that when thoughts are conveyed to your subconscious mind, impressions are made in the brain cells. As soon as your subconscious accepts any idea, it proceeds to put it into effect immediately. It works by association of ideas and uses every bit of knowledge that you have gathered in your lifetime to bring about its purpose. It draws on the infinite power, energy, and wisdom within you. It lines up all the laws of nature to get its way. Sometimes it seems to bring about an immediate solution to your difficulties, but at other times it may take days, weeks, or longer.

Conscious and subconscious terms differentiated

You must remember that these are not two minds. They are merely two spheres of activity within one mind. Your conscious mind is the reasoning mind. It is that phase of mind which chooses. For example, you choose your books, your home, and your partner in life. You make all your decisions with your conscious mind. On the other hand, without any conscious choice on your part, your heart is kept functioning automatically, and the process of digestion, circulation, and breathing are carried on by your subconscious mind through processes independent of your conscious control.

Your subconscious mind accepts what is impressed upon it or what you consciously believe. It does not reason things out like your conscious mind, and it does not argue with you controversially. Your subconscious mind is like the soil which accepts any kind of seed, good or bad. Your thoughts are active and might be likened unto seeds. Negative, destructive thoughts continue to work negatively in your subconscious mind, and in due time will come forth into outer experience which corresponds with them.

A Chinese proverb:

All of the flowers of all the tomorrows lie in the seeds of today
(as do the weeds)
Which do you water all day long?

Remember, your subconscious mind does not engage in proving whether your thoughts are good or bad, true or false, but it responds according to the nature of your thoughts or suggestions. For example, if you consciously assume something as true, even though it may be false, your subconscious mind will accept it as true and proceed to bring about results which must necessarily follow, because you consciously assumed it to be true.

The tremendous power of suggestion

You must realize by now that your conscious mind is the "watchman at the gate," and its chief function is to protect your subconscious mind from false impressions. You are now aware of one of the basic laws of mind: Your subconscious mind is amenable to suggestion. As you know, your subconscious mind does not make comparisons, or contrasts, neither does it reason and think things out for itself. This latter function belongs to your conscious mind. It simply reacts to the impressions given to it by your conscious mind. It does not show a preference for one course of action over another.

The dictionary says that a suggestion is the act or instance of putting something into one's mind, the mental process by which the thought or idea suggested is entertained, accepted, or put into effect.

*Lee Pulos, Ph.D., ABPP, who wrote the Foreword to this book, is a practicing clinical psychologist and hypnotherapist in Vancouver, B.C., Canada. I have been in workshops with Lee where he will put a participant in a light trance and then start to prick his hand with a pin. He tells the subject that he is injecting a numbing substance into his hand. "Your hand is getting very numb," he tells him repeatedly until the subject states he can't feel anything on his hand. To test the "numbness," Lee will give the participant a good pinch. "Can't feel a thing." Then the subject is invited to stick the pin clear through the skin on his hand with the further suggestions, "There will be no pain, no bleeding, and no infection." The participant then sticks the pin (not sterilized) through his hand and per the power of the instructions given to the subconscious, he/she feels **no** pain, there is **no** bleeding (not even a drop) and **no** infection ensues. This is pretty amazing! I know because I have been that "subject."*

I have seen subjects under hypnosis be told that a piece of chalk is a lit cigarette. The hypnotist then touches the subject on the skin of his arm. The subject recoils as though he was actually touched with a lit cigarette. But, what happens next is even harder to believe. A red welt appears on the arm which becomes an actual "heat blister," even though the only thing that touched the subject's arm was the blunt end of a piece of chalk!

*Many of you have heard of, observed, or even participated in "fire walks"
where, through the repetition of strong suggestions to the participants, the
skin on their feet will be "protected" as they walk over red-hot coals. I have
seen this ritual performed many times including native Fijians standing on
molten white-hot rocks for several seconds with no feeling of the heat or any
burning sensation.*

*As a point of disclaimer, I have also seen where, occasionally, a participant
will actually experience a burn on their feet. But, in every such instance they
confessed they had "great doubt" that they would be safe from being burned.*

*Imagine unleashing that same power to more easily help us to achieve
our goals and the things we truly want in our lives. Imagine being able to
turn off the switch of that little voice that likes to constantly remind us of
our doubts and fears. Imagine that same power used to proactively manage
our health and physical well-being. That's where we are headed as we move
forward with this work.*

The subconscious cannot reason like your conscious mind

Your subconscious mind cannot argue controversially. Hence, if you give
it wrong suggestions, it will accept them as true and will proceed to bring
them to pass as conditions, experiences, and events. All things that have
happened to you are based on thoughts impressed on your subconscious
mind through belief. If you have conveyed erroneous concepts to your
subconscious mind, the sure method of overcoming them is by the repetition of constructive, harmonious thoughts frequently repeated which
your subconscious mind accepts, thus forming new and healthy habits of
thought and life, for your subconscious mind is the seat of habit.

The constructive and destructive power of suggestion

Some illustrations and comments on heterosuggestion: Heterosuggestion
means suggestions from another person. In all ages the power of sugges-

tion has played a part in the life and thought of man in every period of time and in each country of the earth. In many parts of the world it is the controlling power in religion.

Suggestion may be used to discipline and control ourselves, but it can also be used to take control and command over others who do not know the laws of mind. In its constructive form it is wonderful and magnificent. In its negative aspects it is one of the most destructive of all the response patterns of the mind, resulting in patterns of misery, failure, suffering, sickness, and disaster.

Unless, as an adult, you use constructive autosuggestion, which is a reconditioning therapy, the impressions made on you in the past can cause behavior patterns that cause failure in your personal and social life. Autosuggestion is a means releasing you from the mass of negative verbal conditioning that might otherwise distort your life pattern, making the development of good habits difficult.

*Another word for autosuggestion is **Affirmation**. We define affirmation as:*

"A statement of fact or belief, positive or negative, that tends to lead you toward the end result you expect."

Two things are important here:

1. *The "statement of fact or belief" may be completely true or completely erroneous (but believed to be true). As written by Dr. Murphy just above:*

   Your subconscious mind cannot argue controversially. Hence if you give it wrong suggestions, it will accept them as true and will proceed to bring them to pass as conditions, experiences, and events. All things that have happened to you are based on thoughts impressed on your subconscious mind through belief."

Any statement that follows the words "I am _____" is an affirmation. "I am lousy at (you can fill in the blank)" is an instruction to the subconscious to bring that statement into reality. Likewise, the statement (i.e., affirmation), "I am really good at _____" causes the subconscious to bring that belief into reality.

As Bruce H. Lipton, Ph.D., writes in Spontaneous Evolution:*

Our minds actively co-create the world we experience. Consequently, by changing our beliefs, we have an opportunity to affect world change .

The fact that the mind of the observer influences the outcome of experiments is one of the most profound insights introduced by quantum mechanics. This new physics acknowledges that we are not merely passive observers of our world but, rather we are active participants in its unfolding. . . . Quantum physics has absolutely verified that information processed by our minds influences the shape of the world in which we live.

This is very profound! When Dr. Murphy wrote his book in 1963, a reader had to make the choice of whether he/she believed what Dr. Murphy taught. Although Dr. Murphy **knew** *what he taught was true, he couldn't prove it through scientific analysis. Therefore, the disbelievers took on the role of "victims" and stayed stuck in their same old B.S. (Belief Systems). Those who embraced and practiced the principles taught by Dr. Murphy were labeled "optimists" or just plain "lucky."*

Today, students of this material can eliminate the need to believe or disbelieve as any inquiring mind can find the scientific evidence to validate its veracity.

Thank you, Dr. Bruce Lipton.

2. ***The law of expectations.*** *Seldom does an individual exceed his/her expectations. Remember, an affirmation is "a statement of fact or belief, positive or negative, that tends to lead you toward the end result you* **expect.***" It doesn't read, "The end result that you* **want.***" We don't get what we want, we get what we expect. High-performance people develop high expectations which they hold firmly in their minds as though this picture (or goal) is already achieved.*

You see and feel what you expect to see and feel. The world as you know it is a picture of your expectations. The world as the race of man knows it is the materialization en masse of your individual expectations.

*The Nature of Personal Reality,*** by Jane Roberts

Lipton, op. cit., p. 3.
**Roberts, Jane, The Nature of Personal Reality. *Amber-Allen Pub., New World Library,* 1994

If you want to enhance your performance or alter your behavior in any area of your life, you must simultaneously embrace the mental picture of that accomplishment and hold it tight to you as an imagined end result.

Don't let lower expectations become the lid on the box that holds you down and sabotages your efforts to achieve new goals.

You can counteract negative suggestions

Pick up the newspaper any day, and you can read dozens of items that could sow the seeds of futility, fear, worry, anxiety, and impending doom. If accepted by you, these thoughts of fear could cause you to lose the will for life. Knowing that you can reject all these negative suggestions by giving your subconscious mind constructive autosuggestions, you counteract all these destructive ideas.

Check regularly on the negative suggestions that people make to you. You do not have to be influenced by destructive heterosuggestion.

The suggestions of others in themselves have absolutely no power whatever over you except the power that you give them through your own thoughts. You have to give your mental consent; you have to entertain the thought. Then, it becomes your thought, and you do the thinking. Remember, you have the capacity to choose. Choose life! Choose love! Choose health!

The subconscious does not argue controversially

Your subconscious mind is all-wise and knows the answers to all questions. It does not argue with you or talk back to you. It does not say, "You must not impress me with that." For example, when you say, "I can't do this," "I am too old now," "I can't meet this obligation," "I don't know the right politician," you are impregnating your subconscious with these negative thoughts, and it responds accordingly. You are actually blocking your own good, thereby bringing lack, limitation, and frustration into your life.

When you are seeking an answer to a problem, your subconscious will respond, but it expects you to come to a decision and to a true judgment in your conscious mind. You must acknowledge the answer is in your subconscious mind. However, if you say, "I don't think there is any way out; I am all mixed up and confused; why don't I get an answer?" you are neutralizing your desire.

Still the wheels of your mind, relax, let go, and quietly affirm: "My subconscious knows the answer. It is responding to me now. I give thanks because I know the infinite intelligence of my subconscious knows all things and is revealing the perfect answer to me now."

Review of highlights

1. Think good, and good follows. Think evil, and evil follows. You are what you think about all day long.
2. Your subconscious mind does not argue with you. It accepts what your conscious mind decrees. If you say, "I can't afford it," it may be true, but do not say it. Select a better thought, decree, "I'll buy it. I accept it in my mind."
3. You have the power to choose. Choose health and happiness. You can choose to be friendly, or you can choose to be unfriendly. Choose to be cooperative, joyous, friendly, lovable, and the whole world will respond. This is the best way to develop a wonderful personality.
4. Your conscious mind is the "watchman at the gate." Its chief function is to protect your subconscious mind from false impressions. Choose to believe that something good can happen and is happening now. Your greatest power is your capacity to choose. Choose happiness and abundance.
5. The suggestions and statements of others have no power to hurt you. The only power is the movement of your own thought. You can choose to reject the thoughts or statements of others and affirm the good. You have the power to choose how you will react.

This is very important. Too often we "idolize" certain key figures in our lives who may have good intentions for our well-being, but often underestimate the power their words have upon us. Especially when we are small children. A parent who says in frustration, "What's the matter with you, any-

way!" doesn't understand the impact such a "statement of fact or belief" may have upon the child.

As we begin to fully learn and understand Dr. Murphy's teachings, we can take direct control of our lives and liberate ourselves from the negative influence of others' misdirected comments. We can simply smile inwardly and say, "I am not accepting that destructive criticism because the truth is I am (and we describe the condition we choose for our healthy, happy life)."

In truth, the words of others have no power over us. It is only how we choose to interpret the words with our own self talk that influences or "instructs" our subconscious.

6. Watch what you say. You have to account for every idle word. Never say, "I will fail; I will lose my job; I can't pay the rent." Your subconscious cannot take a joke. It brings all these things to pass.

7. Your mind is not evil. No force of nature is evil. It depends how you use the powers of nature. Use your mind to bless, heal, and inspire all people everywhere.

8. Never say, "I can't." Overcome that fear by substituting the following, "I can do all things through the power of my own subconscious mind."

9. Begin to think from the standpoint of the eternal truths and principles of life and not from the standpoint of fear, ignorance, and superstition. Do not let others do your thinking for you. Choose your own thoughts and make your own decisions.

10. You are the captain of your soul (subconscious mind) and the master of your fate. Remember, you have the capacity to choose. Choose life! Choose love! Choose health! Choose happiness!

11. Whatever your conscious mind assumes and believes to be true, your subconscious mind will accept and bring to pass. Believe in good fortune, divine guidance, right action, and all the blessings of life.

Key 2

SELF TALK

Understanding The Incredible
Power of Your Own Self Talk.

3

Self Talk

There may be nothing more powerful that affects our behavior and effectiveness than our own self talk. The power of our self talk largely determines the results of our endeavors, positively or negatively.

We talk to ourselves at the rate of 150–300 words a minute—or 50,000 thoughts a day!

We are either drugging our mind all day long with negative thoughts (which releases stress hormones) or drugging our mind with positive thoughts (which release "feel good" hormones: dopamine—serotonin—beta endorphins).

As small children we simply spoke out loud. I remember coming home from work one night and going up to my youngest son's bedroom to see him before he went to bed. As I approached the door to his room I heard all this chatter and commotion. I assumed one or more of his friends or siblings were in his room with him. When I came to the doorway, I saw him sitting on the floor with his back to me playing with several of his stuffed animals. He was having a grand time engaged in an enthusiastic and animated conversation. But the voice of each animal was my son. He was enjoying a real life (to him) experience with his animal friends.

As adults we have learned to keep these dialogues internalized although from time to time we may surprise ourselves by blurting our thoughts out loud, even though we may be alone at the time. And we have all observed people alone in their cars apparently involved in expressive conversations with themselves (of course, these were more recognizable prior to cell phones).

When we are talking with others we are concurrently experiencing an internal streaming dialogue interpreting what the other person is saying, preparing our own response while still "listening" to the person doing the talking.

The most powerful dialogues, however, are those dialogues we have with ourselves when we are alone. It is the dialogue of judgments and assessments where we praise ourselves for something we did well or beat ourselves up for something we did poorly.

At the beginning of this chapter I said, "There may be nothing more powerful that affects our behavior and effectiveness than our own self talk." How can that be?

Our self talk is what has created, and continues to create, our self concept.

In The Power of Now,* *author Eckhart Tolle discusses self talk in a section he entitles, "Freeing Yourself From Your Mind."*

Tolle writes,

What exactly do you mean by "watching the thinker?" When someone goes to the doctor and says, "I hear a voice in my head," he or she will most likely be sent to a psychiatrist. The fact is that, in a very similar way, virtually everyone hears a voice, or several voices, in their head all the time: the involuntary thought process that you don't realize you have the power to stop. Continuous monologues or dialogues.

You have probably come across "mad" people in the street incessantly talking or muttering to themselves. Well, that's not much different from what you and all other "normal" people do, except that you don't do it out loud. The voice comments, speculates, judges, compares, complains, likes, dislikes, and so on. The voice isn't necessarily relevant to the situation you find yourself in at the time; it may be reviving the recent or distant past or rehearsing or imagining possible future situations. Here it often imagines things going wrong and negative outcomes; this is called worry. Sometimes this soundtrack is accompanied by visual images or "mental movies." Even if the voice is relevant to the situation at hand, it will interpret it in terms of the past. This is because the voice belongs to your conditioned mind, which is the result of all your past history as well as of the collective cultural mind-set you inherited. So you see and judge the present through the eyes of the past and get a totally distorted view of it. It is not uncommon for the voice to be a person's own worst enemy. Many people live with a tormentor in their head that continuously attacks and punishes them and drains them of vital energy. It is the cause of untold misery and unhappiness, as well as disease.

The good news is that you can free yourself from your mind. This is the only true liberation. You can take the first step right

Tolle, Eckhart. The Power of Now. New *World Library, 2004*

now. Start listening to the voice in your head as often as you can. Pay particular attention to any repetitive thought patterns, those old gramophone records that have been playing in your head perhaps for many years. This is what I mean by "watching the thinker."

As "authority figures" in young people's lives (e.g., parents, coaches, teachers, older siblings), we need to be mindful of how we speak about the performance of a child when they perform in a way that disappoints us. It could be a piano recital, an examination, a sporting event, or whatever. Children are so impressionable that they take literally how their parents might "judge" their performance.

What should we do as a parent, a coach, or a teacher when our child performs less than his or her potential or worse than they normally perform? Obviously, we should create a "picture" in their minds which is consistent with how we envision them, i.e., "Son, I'm sorry that wasn't your best game. I remember having a game like that once myself. You are really a great player and next week you will probably have your best game!"

Or, "Honey, you play that song so well at home over and over. I'll bet you can't wait for your next recital to show everyone how good you are."

As young people our self talk is greatly influenced by the input we receive from those we value and love the most. And as we will see in the next chapter, it is our self talk that forms our self concept.

By the time we reach "adulthood" (i.e., become teenagers) we have pretty firm opinions about what we are good at, bad at, what we like, don't like, kinds of people we like to be around, kinds of people we try to avoid, etc., etc. We accept as "fact" that this is simply the way we are (and are always going to be). In essence we become prisoners of our own data, which we erroneously accept as fact. And since most of us have never been taught how to make constructive changes in our behavior, we proceed with life as if we were on autopilot.

*In conclusion, our Self Talk forms our Self Concept. Our Self Concept determines our Level of Performance. Since we generally perform consistently with our self concept, after such performance we talk to ourselves about the performance, which reinforces our self concept insuring we will continue to perform at the same **level**.*

Our self talk is like a radio station in our brain. Are we listening to the right channel? Should we change channels? Do we know how? Stay tuned! (Pun intended)

We will now discover how our self talk creates our self concept.

Key 3

SELF CONCEPT

Understanding how your Self Concept is the regulating mechanism that determines your Level of Performance in every area of your Life..

4

How Our Self Talk Develops
Our Self Concept

In this chapter we will learn how our self concept is formed and the incredible influence it has on the decisions we make and the result(s) of such decisions. It begins and ends with our understanding of the power of our self concept and the realization that the self concept is the regulating mechanism that determines our level of performance in any area of our lives, positive or negative.

We are very complex, multifaceted beings who, like the many conveniences we enjoy in everyday life, have other mechanisms and tools available to us that are simply not taught in our schools. Therefore, many of us go through life totally unaware of how we became who we are, but more important, how we have the capacity to make constructive changes in any area(s) of our lives that may not be working as well as we would desire. Simply put, most people don't know how to change. Therefore, they resolve themselves to an internal mantra of "that's just the way I am," grateful for their blessings while accepting that they simply drew the short straw for all of their shortcomings. And, this is how they live out the rest of their life.

As we "de-hypnotize" ourselves from our negative belief "trances" and our limiting cultural trances and "re-hypnotize" ourselves with new beliefs, i.e., affirmations (See chapter 8), we can expand the bandwidth of our brain into new area codes with no static compared to the static of the old area code.

Let's peel back the onion and examine how we became "that's just the way I am!"

Our first two years

At birth we are born with pure potential. By that I mean we have no data that suggests we can't do anything. Our first two years are among the most dynamic growth years of our life. Since we are non-verbal, our parents can't tell us what we can't do or that we are growing too fast. In that first two years we learn to walk, to dress ourselves, feed ourselves and begin to develop language. Although we have a very small vocabulary, we begin to understand what mom and dad are telling us and are talking to us about.

Our brain speaks five electrical languages

The following I learned from Dr. Lee Pulos in one of his workshops:

> From birth to age 2 our brainwaves are primarily DELTA (1.5–4 hertz) Between the ages of 2 and 6 our brainwaves speed up a bit to THETA (4–8 hertz). Between ages 6 and 12 our brainwaves speed up again to ALPHA (8–12 hertz). Then from 12 on, BETA (12–40 hertz).

> What happens when someone is hypnotized? Their brainwaves slow to THETA/ALPHA (the optimal hypnotic state is 7.3 hertz)
> Thus, between the ages of 2 and 12 we are in the most hypnotizable-programmable brainwave states known to man. Why? Isn't this when our beliefs are programmed and the roots of our self esteem and self concept are laid down? Thus, as we de-hypnotize ourselves from our negative belief trances with new affirmations, we create more empowering belief trances.
> The fifth electrical language is GAMMA seen in high-performance states (40–200 hertz).

We learn from two sources

As small children, we primarily learn from two sources.

1. We learn by imitating one or both of our parents. Why? Our parents are our primary source of love. As small children, we need so much love that we will behave in such a manner as we believe will please mom or dad. We seem to get "rewarded" when we make them happy.
2. We move toward comfort and away from discomfort.

The bottom line is we come into the world as a totally empty vessel. We do, however, seem to have an insatiable curiosity and desire to learn. By the age of two we have learned some words and we quickly begin to develop our base or primary language. Almost all our data input is provided by our parents and older siblings. They share with us THEIR opinions of what is good or *bad, right or wrong, and how we should behave ("good girl") or shouldn't be-have ("bad boy"). By the time we are six years old, we have developed some pretty strong opinions of who we are, what our world (family and friends) is all about, and we have even begun to have some early thoughts about what areas we may be good at or areas we are not good at.*

IMPORTANT: NONE OF THIS HAS ANYTHING TO DO WITH WHO WE REALLY ARE, BUT RATHER EVERYTHING TO DO WITH WHO WE THINK WE ARE OR SHOULD BECOME.

We didn't come into the world with any predisposed thoughts about being a Catholic or a Protestant, a Republican or a Democrat, a doctor or a lawyer, etc. Most of the data about who and what we are is "inherited" in the beliefs (not necessarily facts or truths) of our parents, siblings, teachers, coaches and all those authoritative "role models" who as children, especially as small children, we look at with awe. Since we have no contrary data, we accept what they tell us as the **TRUTH**. *By age six we are in school and now have additional teachers and coaches who help us clarify even further who we are and what we are good or not good at.*

We have already introduced the notion of self talk, so with our own self talk we reinforce what we were told or experienced.

It is our self talk that creates and determines our self concept(s). So, it isn't what mom or dad or others said to us that creates our self concept, but how we interpret what others said and how we feel about what was said. As we will learn, the purpose of language is to create or access an image or picture in our mind. Those pictures most often are accompanied by feelings or emotions. So, our own internal dialog creates pictures and feelings that are stored in the subconscious area of our mind and that influence our future behaviors. We will discuss this in depth in Chapter 7.

The following is from Outwitting the Devil: The Secret to Freedom and Success *by Napoleon Hill.**

Have you ever heard a parent finish a child's sentence? Or seen a parent complete a child's homework? Remember those science fairs at school where it is obvious the kids had a lot of outside "help" with their science projects? Mom and Dad may have "helped" a little too much, but deep down they know that their child appreciates the help and recognizes what great parents they

*Hill, Napoleon. Annotated by Sharon L. Lechter. Outwitting the Devil: The Secret to Freedom and Success. Sterling. 2011 are. Right? Actually, the child may be thinking, "Mom and Dad don't think I can do it on my own . . . so why bother!" Eventually this parental "help" will destroy the child's self-confidence. By allowing children to be truly in charge, parents will help their kids develop the habit of thinking for themselves!

For now, simply understand that it is our own self talk that forms our self concept. What is our self concept? Our self concept is the way we view ourselves. By definition,

The self concept is the total and averaging of the value judgments placed upon yourself and those that have been placed upon you as children by parents and others---especially as small children in every area of your life.

We have an overall self concept which is "the total and averaging" of multiple individual self concepts.

Individual Self Concepts

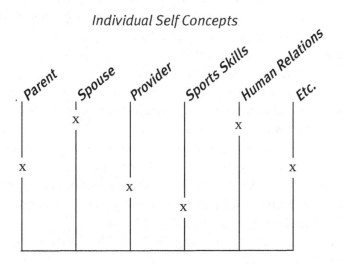

We have hundreds of individual self concepts. Within "sports skills" we may have a high self concept as a skier, a low self concept as a golfer, etc.

THE OPERATING PRINCIPLE HERE IS THAT THE SELF CONCEPT IS THE REGULATING MECHANISM THAT DETERMINES OUR LEVEL OF PERFORMANCE IN EVERY AREA OF OUR LIFE.

There is always a one-to-one relationship between our self concept and our level of performance.

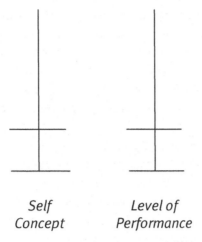

*Self
Concept*

*Level of
Performance*

Most of us have been trained to believe that by working hard on our per-formance, once our performance improves we will allow ourselves to think better of our self in that area of our life. Or, we allow our self concept to im-prove. Fortunately, it doesn't work that way. We are not discounting the value of instruction, training, and practice. But the cause-and-effect relationship is that the self concept drives how we perform.

Let me share an example that vividly illustrates this point.

Prior to 1954 it was believed to be the "truth" among world class runners that it was impossible for man to ever run the mile in less than four minutes. Since man had first invented the stop watch and for tens of thousands of races over decades, no one had ever been timed in running the mile under four minutes. Men had come dangerously close, within tenths of a second, but no one had broken the four minute barrier.

And then what happened?

In 1954 a medical student from Great Britain, Roger Bannister, became the first runner in history to run the mile in under four minutes. So what? So what is that over the next 3 years, 16 others had run more than 40 sub-four-minute miles. There was no change in the equipment (in this case run-ning shoes or the surface of the running track), there was no breakthrough in technique or training methodology, there was simply the removal of the **self imposed** limitation that it was "impossible" to ever run the mile in under four minutes.

Participating in sports activities are good examples of people perform-ing consistently with their self concept.

In the sport of baseball, the hitters have a batting average and the pitchers have an earned run average. And, most of the time the players' results are consistent with their average, or self concept. When they perform better than their "average" (self concept), they are said to be "in the zone." When their performance is less than their average, we say they are in a slump. The same is true with golfers whose scores are consistent with their handicap (interesting word).

Why is it we sabotage our success when we start performing so much better than our self concept? Because our self concept, as we have said, is the regulating factor that determines our level of performance.

Remember, our self concept is how we view ourselves in any area of our lives. And, when we change the picture (positive or negative), we change the result of our performance (positive or negative).

If we want to improve our level of performance, we need to raise our self concept.

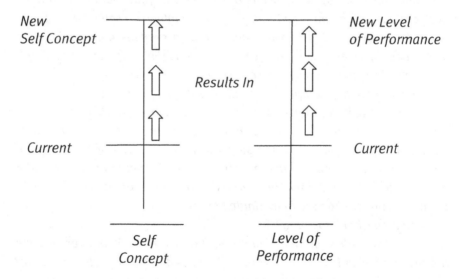

We have all developed conditioned responses that inhibit our ability to become all that we truly are. As we proceed through this book we will show you techniques to take personal inventory of what you like or don't like about yourself; what you believe yourself to be good or bad at; and to recognize certain behavioral patterns that you might want to change. As we identify the things we would like to change or have different in our lives, we will then learn step-by-step procedures and proven techniques that will enable us to

bring about changes more effortlessly than we could have ever imagined. "Change" is not a dirty word and doesn't have to be accompanied by the discomfort we have been conditioned to believe must occur.

Now let's look more deeply at the enormous power of our subconscious mind and then move into a better understanding of the relationship between our conscious and subconscious mind.

5

The Miracle-Working Power
of Your Subconscious

The power of your subconscious is enormous. It inspires you, it guides you, and it reveals to you names, facts, and scenes from the storehouse of memory. Your subconscious started your heartbeat, controls the circulation of your blood, and regulates your digestion, assimilation, and elimination. When you eat a piece of bread, your subconscious mind transmutes it into tissue, muscle, bone, and blood. This process is beyond the knowledge of the wisest man who walks the earth. Your subconscious mind controls all the vital processes and functions of your body and knows the answer to all problems.

Your subconscious mind never sleeps, never rests. It is always on the job. You can discover the miracle-working power of your subconscious by plainly stating to your subconscious prior to sleep that you wish a certain specific thing accomplished. You will be delighted to discover that forces within you will be released, leading to the desired result. Here, then, is a source of power and wisdom which places you in touch with omnipotence or the power that moves the world, guides the planets in their course, and causes the sun to shine.

Your subconscious mind is the source of your ideals, aspirations, and altruistic urges. It was through the subconscious mind that Shakespeare perceived great truths hidden from the average man of his day. Undoubtedly, it was the response of his subconscious mind that caused the Greek sculptor Phidias to portray beauty, order, symmetry, and proportion in marble and bronze. It enabled the Italian artist Raphael to paint Madonnas, and Ludwig van Beethoven to compose symphonies.

Your subconscious is your Book of Life

Whatever thoughts, beliefs, opinions, theories, or dogmas you write, engrave, or impress on your subconscious mind, you shall experience them as the objective manifestation of circumstances, conditions, and events. What you write on the inside, you will experience on the outside. You have two sides to your life, objective and subjective, visible and invisible, thought and its manifestation.

Your thought is received by your brain, which is the organ of your conscious reasoning mind. When your conscious or objective mind accepts the thought completely, it is sent to the solar plexus, called the brain of your mind, where it becomes flesh and is made manifest in your experience.

Your subconscious cannot argue. It acts only from what you write on it. It accepts your verdict or the conclusions of your conscious mind as final. This is why you are always writing on the book of life, because your thoughts become your experiences. The American essayist Ralph Waldo Emerson said, "Man is what he thinks about all day long."

What Is Impressed In The Subconscious Is Expressed

William James, the father of American psychology, said that the power to move the world is in your subconscious mind. Your subconscious mind is one with infinite intelligence and boundless wisdom. It is fed by hidden springs, and is called the law of life. Whatever you impress upon your subconscious mind, the latter will move heaven and earth to bring it to pass. You must, therefore, impress it with right ideas and constructive thoughts.

The reason there is so much chaos and misery in the world is because people do not understand the interaction of their conscious and subconscious minds. When these two principles work in accord, in concord, in peace, and synchronously together, you will have health, happiness, peace and joy. There is no sickness or discord when the conscious and subconscious work together harmoniously and peacefully.

Whatever is impressed in your subconscious mind is expressed on the screen of space. This same truth was proclaimed by Moses, Isaiah,

Jesus, Buddha, Zoroaster, Lao-tzu, and all the illumined seers of the ages. Whatever you feel as true subjectively is expressed as conditions, experiences, and events. Motion and emotion must balance. This is the great law of life.

You will find throughout all nature the law of action and reaction, of rest and motion. These two must balance, then there will be harmony and equilibrium. You are here to let the life principle flow through you rhythmically and harmoniously. The intake and the outgo must be equal. The impression and the expression must be equal. All your frustration is due to unfulfilled desire. *(An uncompleted act creates frustration.)*

What is your idea or feeling about yourself now? Every part of your being expresses that idea. Your vitality, body, financial status, friends, and social status represent a perfect reflection of the idea you have of yourself. This is the real meaning of what is impressed in your subconscious mind, and which is expressed in all phases of your life.

We injure ourselves by the negative ideas which we entertain. How often have you wounded yourself by getting angry, fearful, jealous, or vengeful? These are the poisons that enter your subconscious mind. You were not born with these negative attitudes. Feed your subconscious mind life-giving thoughts, and you will wipe out all the negative patterns lodged therein. As you continue to do this, all the past will be wiped out and remembered no more.

How the subconscious controls all functions of the body

While you are awake or sound asleep upon your bed, the ceaseless, tireless action of your subconscious mind controls all the vital functions of your body without the help of your conscious mind. For example, while you are asleep your heart continues to beat rhythmically, your lungs do not rest, and the process of inhalation and exhalation, whereby your blood absorbs fresh air, goes on just the same as when you are awake. Your subconscious controls your digestive processes and glandular secretions, as well as all the other mysterious operations of your body. The hair on your face continues to grow whether you are asleep or awake. Scientists tell us that the skin secretes much more perspiration during sleep than during the waking hours. Your eyes, ears, and other senses are active during sleep. For instance, many of our great scientists have received answers to perplexing problems while they were asleep. They saw the answers in a dream *(we will discuss how this happens in detail in Chapter 13).*

In his New York Times bestselling book The Brain That Changes Itself,* *author Norman Doidge, M.D. writes:*

> The newest brain scans show that when we dream, that part of the brain that processes emotion, and our sexual survival, and aggressive instincts, is quite active. At the same time the prefrontal cortex system, which is responsible for inhibiting our emotions and instincts, shows lower activity. With instincts turned up and inhibitions turned down, the dreaming brain can reveal impulses that are normally blocked from awareness.
>
> Scores of studies show that sleep affects plastic change by allowing us to consolidate learning and memory. When we learn a skill during the day, we will be better at it the next day if we have a good night's sleep. "Sleeping on a problem" often does make sense.

Oftentimes your conscious mind interferes with the normal rhythm of the heart, lungs, and functioning of the stomach and intestines by worry, anxiety, fear, and depression. These patterns of thought interfere with the harmonious functioning of your subconscious mind. When mentally disturbed, the best procedure is to let go, relax, and still the wheels of your thought processes. Speak to your subconscious mind, telling it to take over in peace, harmony and divine order. You will find that all the functions of your body will become normal again. Be sure to speak to your subconscious mind with authority and conviction, and it will conform to your command.

Your subconscious seeks to preserve your life and restore you to health at all costs. It causes you to love your children which also illustrates an instinctive desire to preserve all life. Let us suppose you accidentally ate some bad food. Your subconscious mind would cause you to regurgi-

Doidge, Norman. The Brain That Changes Itself: Stories of Personal Triumph from the Frontiers of Brain Science. *Penguin. 2007.*

tate it. If you inadvertently took some poison, your subconscious powers would proceed to neutralize it. If you completely entrusted yourself to its wonder-working power, you would be entirely restored to health.

How to convey the idea of perfect health to your subconscious mind

A wonderful way to convey the idea of health to your subconscious is through disciplined or scientific imagination. I told a man who was suffering from functional paralysis to make a vivid picture of himself walking around in his office, touching the desk, answering the telephone, and doing all the things he ordinarily would do if he were healed. I explained to him that this idea and mental picture of perfect health would be accepted by his subconscious mind.

He lived the role and actually felt himself back in the office. He knew that he was giving his subconscious mind something definite to work upon. His subconscious mind was the film upon which the picture was impressed. One day, after several weeks of frequent conditioning of the mind with this mental picture, the telephone rang by prearrangement and kept ringing while his wife and nurse were out. The telephone was about twelve feet away, but nevertheless he managed to answer it. He was healed at that hour. The healing power of his subconscious mind responded to his mental imagery, and a healing followed.

This man had a mental block which prevented impulses from the brain reaching his legs, therefore, he said he could not walk. When he shifted his attention to the healing power within him, the power flowed through his focused attention, enabling him to walk.

⊳Ideas worth remembering

1. Your subconscious mind controls all the vital processes of your body and knows the answer to all problems.
2. Prior to sleep, turn over a specific request to your subconscious mind and prove its miracle-working power to yourself.

3. Whatever you impress on your subconscious mind is expressed on the screen of space as conditions, experiences, and events. Therefore, you should carefully watch all ideas and thoughts entertained in your conscious mind.

4. The law of action and reaction is universal. Your thought is action, and the reaction is the automatic response of your subconscious mind to your thought. Watch your thoughts!

5. All frustration is due to unfulfilled desires. If you dwell on obstacles, delays, and difficulties, your subconscious mind responds accordingly, and you are blocking you own good.

6. The Life Principle will flow through you rhythmically and harmoniously if you consciously affirm: "I believe that the subconscious power which gave me this desire is now fulfilling it through me." This dissolves all conflicts.

7. You can interfere with the normal rhythm of your heart, lungs, and other organs by worry, anxiety, and fear. Feed your subconscious with thoughts of harmony, health, and peace, and all the functions of your body will become normal again.

8. Keep your conscious mind busy with the expectation of the best, and your subconscious will faithfully reproduce your habitual thinking.

9. Imagine the happy ending or solution to your problem, feel the thrill of accomplishment, and what you imagine and feel will be accepted by your subconscious mind and bring it to pass.

6

Habit Patterns: First We Form Habits, Then They Form Us

*Let me repeat the subtitle to this chapter: "First We Form Habits, Then They Form Us." Just like our self concept, we came into the world with no formed habits. All of our habits have been developed, and once developed most often become conditioned responses to our environment and internal perceptions. It is important to note that maintaining a habit is our choice. For those habits that support us and serve us well, we need to apply purposeful practice and attention. But, more important, we have the capacity to change **any** habit that may no longer be useful or of benefit to us.*

We have two types of habit patterns---positive and negative. Positive habit patterns may include walking, talking, eating, driving our car or a thousand other things. Negative habit patterns always contain the element of FEAR. We will talk more about negative habit patterns later in this chapter.

Habit patterns are wonderful because they allow us to do so many things simultaneously. Since we can only hold one thought at a time in our conscious mind, without habit patterns it would be difficult (dangerous?) to attempt simultaneous activities.

Let's take driving a car, for example. When you first started driving, you didn't just jump in the car, turn on the ignition, shift into drive, release the brake and take off. You didn't know what to do. So with a good instructor (mom and/ or dad) combined with driver's education, you learned how to drive an automobile. But, it took some time, some mistakes, and a lot of concentration. On your first few attempts you weren't about to simultaneously get on your cell phone or listen to books on tape. It was all you could do to avoid oversteering, braking too hard, and how about those first few attempts at parallel parking on a steep hill! (My daughters, Julie and Jill, may still be upset with me for that drill.)

O.K. You get the drift. We learn or develop habits through:

1. *Data input; and,*
2. *Repetition*

Here's what this means neurologically. In his book The Talent Code,* *author Daniel Coyle writes:*

> The talent code is built on revolutionary scientific discoveries involving a neural insulator called myelin, which some neurologists now consider to be the holy grail of acquiring skill. Here's why. Every human skill, whether it's playing baseball or playing Bach, is created by chains of nerve fibers carrying a tiny electrical impulse— basically, a signal traveling through a circuit. Myelin's vital role is to wrap those nerve fibers the same way that rubber insulation wraps a copper wire, making the signal stronger and faster by preventing the electrical impulses from leaking out. When we fire our circuits the right way—when we practice swinging that bat or playing that note—our myelin responds by wrapping layers of insulation around that neural circuit, each new layer adding a bit more skill and speed. The thicker the myelin gets, the better it insulates, and the faster and more accurate our movements and thoughts become.

Coyle continues:

> The revolution is built on three simple facts. (1) Every human movement, thought, or feeling is a precisely timed electric signal traveling through a chain of neurons—a circuit of nerve fibers. (2) Myelin is the insulation that wraps these nerve fibers and increases signal strength, speed, and accuracy. (3) The more we fire a particular circuit, the more myelin optimizes that circuit, and the stronger, faster, and more fluent our movements and thoughts become.

In our driving example as stated, the data input is the instruction we receive, again from parents, driving school, older siblings, or friends.

The repetition is self explanatory. We simply keep "practicing" (i.e., driving) over and over until it becomes a habit. How do we know when it is a habit? It becomes a habit when we no longer have to think about it consciously. *Our data input, through repetition, is now embedded into the* subconscious *area of our mind. In other words, we simply turn the activity, in this case driving, over to our "auto pilot" (no pun intended) who performs the activity while our conscious mind is free to participate in other activities such as talking with a fellow passenger, or listening to a ball game on the radio. Have you ever been in a restaurant or bar with a piano and observed the pianist playing beautiful mu-*

Coyle, Daniel, The Talent Code. *Bantam: 2009*

sic while fully engaged in a deep conversation with one of the customers. The pianist's hands are flying over the key board without an error while the pianist herself is concentrating on the conversation with the customer. Needless to say, the pianist didn't play the song this competently the first time she attempted to play it. She read the music with great concentration (with no side conversations) and practiced it over and over until she could play the song flawlessly without having to think about it consciously. *It had become a habit pattern.*

In this same example, if another patron asked her to play a song of which she had the sheet music but had not committed the song to memory, she could read the music as she played, but there would be no side-bar conversations as her full concentration would have to be on reading the music.

The same could be said of typing. First we learned to type, with much instruction and many mistakes, and now we just type.

So, as stated previously, habit patterns are great in that they allow us to do so many different things without having to apply conscious thought. But, now we will examine how certain habit patterns, specifically negative habit patterns, can affect our behavior in negative ways and in some instances may actually be harmful to us.

Let me just make one comment about bad *habits. Bad habits are simply "bad habits," those habits one may have developed over time that seem difficult to break even though one wishes to break them. Professionals may label them "addictions." But to rid ourselves of a "bad" habit, we use the same tools and techniques taught in this book to bring about **any** change in your life that you desire (See Chapter 8, "Affirmations and Affirmation Techniques"). The bottom line is, you no longer need to be a "prisoner" of antiquated beliefs, attitudes, or old habits that may be blocking your realization of all that you truly are, not the illusion(s) or delusion of what you have been conditioned to* believe *you are. You will soon learn that liberating yourself from all the junk (also known as "baggage") you have collected along the way does not have to be an arduous task nor require years of contemplation in the presence of a monk on the high plains of Tibet.*

Now about negative habit patterns.

We stated earlier that all negative habit patterns contain the element of fear. And, in most cases our negative habit patterns are imbedded into us before the age of six. Our memory of how we got a negative habit pattern is repressed. And, although we have no conscious memory of how we obtained this "feeling," it does affect our future decisions and behavior. After the age of six, we may develop a fear of something, but the event(s) or data that caused it is still remembered vividly. Thus by our definition, it would not be a "negative habit pattern."

There are two types of negative habit patterns—inhibitive and compulsive.

Inhibitive Negative Habit Patterns

An inhibitive negative habit pattern contains the notion, "I can't do (fill in the blank) or something bad is going to happen to me."

Often times phobias experienced as adults are the result of early childhood traumas in which the memory of such traumas are suppressed. For example, a small child may have a traumatic experience of falling into a swimming pool before learning how to swim. Thinking one might be drowning, at any age, would be incredibly frightening. But, after the age of six one would retain the memory of such an event and not necessarily be traumatized by it or develop a phobia of getting in the water. This small child, however, develops an innate fear of being in the water from one life-threatening event.

As an adult this same person may have a dreadful fear of water, but they don't know why as they have amnesia of this early childhood trauma. They simply have an inhibitive negative habit which creates an internal alarm when they are near water.

"I can't go in the water or something bad is gong to happen to me."

An adult who is claustrophobic may have been accidentally (or intentionally) locked in their bedroom, or a closet, or perhaps stuck in a mal-functioning elevator. To a small child this can be very traumatic. Again, as an adult the memory of the childhood event is suppressed; the adult simply feels great discomfort and perhaps even fear when confined in small places.

"I don't want to go into that small, dark room or something bad is going to happen to me."

These are examples of inhibitive negative habit patterns, both of which contain the element of fear and happened before the age of six.

Dr. Murphy provides tools for overcoming these kinds of fears in Chapter 21 of this book.

Compulsive Negative Habit Patterns

A compulsive negative habit pattern suggests, "I have to do something, or something bad is going to happen to me."

There are many different compulsive negative habit patterns, but the three most common are:

1. *The compulsive punctual*
2. *The compulsive orderly*
3. *The compulsive active*

*Remember, most of these habit patterns were ingrained in us before the age of six. So, let's examine how one might become a compulsive punctual, or, "I **have to** be on time or else (you fill in the blank)." It makes sense that since these behavioral patterns are developed by age six, in most instances they are handed down to us by mom and/or dad (or whoever served in that parental role). It is also important to point out that the parent who "helped" us develop our compulsive negative habit pattern most likely had the **same** habit pattern themselves.*

*Now let's see how young Jimmy became a compulsive punctual before the a6ge of six. As implied above, dad is a raging punctuality freak. He storms around the house (and the office and the Little League teams, etc.) preaching the mantra, "If you can't be on time, be **early**!" Poor little Jimmy hasn't got a chance. He is playing at his friend's house next door at age four and shows up at home 15 minutes late for dinner. The first time he gets the lecture. The second time he gets the threats, i.e., like being sent to his room, or whatever good, loving, compulsive punctual fathers do. And, the third time dad totally loses it! It doesn't take Jimmy very long to "get it." He develops the compulsive negative pattern that says, "I have to be on time or else _____" (and filling in the blank is not a very pleasant picture for a four year old.)*

So here is a clear and realistic example how one develops a negative habit pattern before the age of six and it contains the element of fear. And, you might ask, "So what? How does that affect me as an adult?" Answer: the same way it affected Jimmy's daddy. He did not act rationally, or sane, when it came to the possibility of being late.

Omega founder John Boyle did a lot of work with the San Diego police department. He learned that 80% of the auto accidents in San Diego County were caused by people driving too fast because they were "in a hurry" or "running late for an appointment." Imagine a compulsive punctual on his way to meet his number one customer and thinking that he is going to be late. He will be gripped with illusionary fears that he may lose the customer, and if so, his boss will fire him and his wife will divorce him, etc. He becomes temporarily insane, drives much faster than the speed limit, risks running a red light, and having a terrible accident.

The affirmation for breaking the compulsive grip on being punctual is, *"It is good to be on time, but I don't* have *to be on time."*

We mentioned the other two most common compulsive habit patterns: the compulsive orderly and the compulsive active person. Four year old Mary's mother is a compulsive "neat-nik." She is constantly wandering the house looking for anything that looks out of place or undone. God forbid little Mary may forget to make her bed one day or leave her nightie on the floor. (Dad was probably screaming at all the kids to hurry up and get in the car or they were going to be late for school.) Mom fumes all day waiting for Mary to get home from school because this is the third time she didn't make her bed. You've got the picture.

And, the compulsively active negative habit pattern is created by the parent(s) who just has to be busy doing something all the time. They never just relax or take time out. That household script goes, "Are you just going to sit around the house and watch cartoons all day? Why aren't you reading those books I bought you? (Dad probably doesn't know that little four year old Jimmy or Mary haven't learned to read yet), or practicing your free throws?" And it goes on and on.

The importance and value of identifying your own negative habit patterns is twofold:

1. To eliminate the compulsive hold they have had on you and develop a sense of sane behavior about whatever it is that you **use to** be compulsive about; and,
2. To break the family chain so you don't pass on the same compulsive behavioral patterns to your own children, if or when you should have them.

We have now learned a little bit about how our self concept influences our performance, how our self concept is developed, the benefit and value of positive habits, and the obstacles associated with negative habit patterns.

We are now going to transition into better understanding the conscious and subconscious areas of the mind and how they interact together in determining our choice(s) of action in everything we do. As part of this transition, I would like to share with you an excerpt from an article I read written by Charles T. Tart, Ph.D. In a subsection headed, "Who am I—the Beliefs Experience," Dr. Tart writes:

The many theories or belief systems we have about who we are, such as, "I am a Christian," or "I am a Buddhist," or "I am a sinner," provide yet another perspective. If we hold these theories purely as *theories*—if we say, "I have a certain set of beliefs, and I don't know if they're really true, but I act on them sometimes"— life wouldn't be so bad. The problem is that these theories are thoroughly conditioned into us when we are children, literally automatizing the way we perceive ourselves and the world. We don't act on them "sometimes" or choose to act on them. And the process of enculturation transmits not only the culture's knowledge but also its restrictions.

Our unexamined belief systems control how we live. Jumping ahead to the question of what we can do to live a better life . . . , one thing is to find out what theories have been conditioned into us, acquire some perspective on them, and make some adult decisions about whether to continue to automatically believe them. "Do I want to believe that *that* is who I am?" Let's not confuse the theories we have about ourselves, even though they may run a lot of our life, with who we actually are and what we can find out by direct observation. As I said, from the perspective of cultivated experience, I am *nothing*: I am not a thing but a process that is open to change.*

Thank you, Dr. Tart.

*Tart, Charles T. "What Death Tells Us About Life" Death: Window to the Infinite. No. 17 (2007-2008): 30-35. IONS, Shift In Action.

Key 4

SELF
DIRECTION

Understanding how the data
stored in your Subconscious
Memory Bank largely determines
the decisions you make and how
you behave.

7

Understanding the Relationship Between the Conscious and Subconscious Mind

In Chapter 5, Dr. Murphy wrote:

> The reason there is so much chaos and misery in the world is because people do not understand the interaction of their conscious and subconscious minds. When these two principles work in accord, in concord, in peace, and synchronously together, you will have health, happiness, peace and joy. There is no sickness or discord when the conscious and subconscious work together harmoniously and peacefully.

Now let's look more closely at the interaction between the conscious and subconscious that Dr. Murphy speaks of and how the data stored in our subconscious largely determines the decisions we make and how we behave.

We have three areas of the mind that are the foundation for how we think, how we create, and how we make decisions both consciously and subconsciously. The three areas of the mind are: the conscious, the subconscious, and the supraconscious. These are not three separate minds, but three spheres of our one mind.

When I first attended the Executive Dynamics (later named Omega) seminar in 1969 as referenced in the Introduction to this book, I remember the founder, John Boyle, going up to the blackboard and writing the following three circles on the following page.

This is what I learned from his description of how these areas of the mind interact.

We will begin with the subconscious. One of the primary functions of the subconscious is to store data. It is the area of our mind that records and stores memory. In computer terms we could think of it as our hard drive. And, what is fascinating is everything we have seen, heard, experienced, and how we felt about those experiences, since birth, is all stored in our subconscious or memory bank—everything. And that which we have "forgotten" can be

49

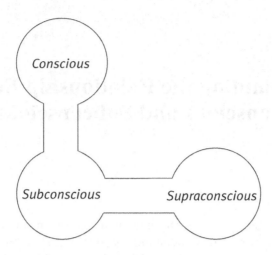

*retrieved through the use of chemicals or age regression hypnosis. Many psy-
chotherapists use hypnosis as a technique of rediscovering early childhood
traumas that may still have a negative or detrimental impact on a person's
behavior as an adult. Powerful phobias and deep rooted fears are often for-
mulated as young children, and when we become adults, we have amnesia
as to where these fears came from; but we know that certain circumstances
or situations trigger what often is very irrational behavior.*

*Additionally, our negative habit patterns are stored in our subconscious.
So, mentally imagine the subconscious as looking like this.*

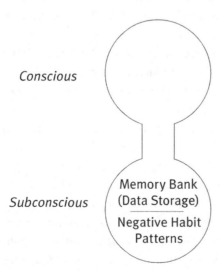

As we will now learn, the data stored in our subconscious largely deter-mines our behavior. And, since none of us have gone through life having had exactly the same experiences, or data input, no two of us can be expected to act exactly the same way. This is often why when we see someone acting completely differently than we would to the same situation, we think they are crazy or something is wrong with THEM. All of our behavior is conditioned by the data we have collected along the way that triggers our response.

At the conscious level, four basic things occur:

1. *We* perceive *incoming stimuli through our senses.*
2. *We go through a process of* comparison *or identification.*
3. *We* analyze *what we have identified.*
4. *We make a* decision *for directed action, reaction, or inaction.*

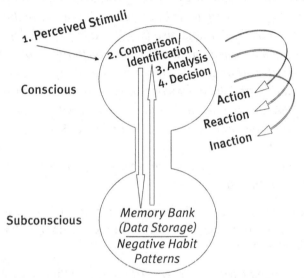

Let's elaborate on each of these functions. We can refer to the following model for ease of reference:

1. **Perception.** *We perceive incoming stimuli in the conscious mind through our senses. We see, hear, feel, smell, or taste something. (We also have many more senses than the Basic Five still being taught in school. For ex-ample, intuition, sense of balance, etc.)*
2. **Comparison.** *We simultaneously go into our subconscious to identify what it is that we are perceiving. Is it a car? An airplane? A boat? A bird? An el-ephant? A certain kind of food? A friend? An enemy? Or is it something we have no data on whatsoever?*

3. **Analysis.** *Once we have retrieved data telling us what it is that we are perceiving, we ask our self, "Is this a good thing? A bad thing? Something that will make me happy? Sad? Comfortable? Uncomfortable?" etc.*

As we wrote earlier, small children learn from primarily two sources:

- *Imitating one or both of their parents (since our parents are our primary source of love, we will do almost anything to gain their approval).*
- *Moving toward that which makes us comfortable or moving away from or avoiding something that may make us uncomfortable.*

4. **Decision.** *Once we have made this internal self-analysis, we make a decision for action, inaction, or reaction.*

So, the bottom line is, we are all making decisions based largely on past experiences we have had or data we have received about something that may or may not be the truth. Our data also includes all of our beliefs, attitudes, and opinions, we have been formulating since birth right up to the present day, many of which may be completely out of date. Many of us become "prisoners" of our data. Our data, or subconscious, is like the hardware that literally "runs us." We all operate on certain programs, but for many, they keep operating the same old programs (i.e., B.S., or "Belief Systems") that may no longer be relevant.

As Eric Hoffer, American author and recipient of the Presidential Medal of Freedom, so beautifully states:

> In a time of change, learners inherit the earth, while the learned find themselves beautifully equipped to deal with a world that no longer exists.

We all know people who allow very little "gray" in their lives. Most everything is black or white. They have very definite opinions about almost everything and very little interest in considering different viewpoints or any new data or information that may cause them to change their view or opinion.

*The learners who "inherit the earth" view education as a continuous life-long process. They are constantly seeking new data, challenging some of their own assumptions, and willing to be introspective in analyzing their subconscious data bank to determine what "programs" may need to be updated and what old data may be erroneous, causing them to make decisions that no longer serve them well. Their egos are in check and the **truth** is more important than being "right."*

Let's look at how three different people may react totally differently to identically the same situation, not based on the truth or reality of the situation, but rather based on their past experiences. Imagine that I am giving a lecture on the subject I am presently writing about. I ask for three volunteers to come onto the stage. Three ladies, Mary, Sally, and Jane volunteer. I ask them to be seated at a round table. I tell them we are going to have a discussion about snakes. We are going to talk about the garter snake. I tell them how the garter snake does not have teeth, cannot bite, and eats insects, not people. I continue by stating there is no rational reason why one should fear a garter snake. Intellectually they all agree. I then say, "Good, as long as we now know there is absolutely no reason to fear a garter snake, let me introduce you to my pet, Larry," and I pull out a live garter snake and drop it on the table.

Before the snake even hits the table, Mary is airborne, letting out an extremely loud scream as she sprints off stage, down the aisle and out the door never to be seen again.

What happened here? OK, let's go through the four things we have just written about.

1. **Perception.** *Mary perceives through her senses, in this case her eyes, an image of something alive, long and slender, and moving in a zigzag pattern.*

2. **Comparison.** *Mary goes to her subconscious (memory bank) and finds some data that quickly tells her this is a "snake."*

3. **Analysis.** *In determining whether this is going to make her comfortable and bring her pleasure or make her uncomfortable, it takes her only a nanosecond to bring up the subconscious recorded picture of that little Jimmy Jensen in the third grade chasing her down the street with a garter snake, which he lovingly drops down the back of her blouse. Mary made a life decision at that point that she is never again going to be this close to a snake. In fact, if she is watching a movie and a snake appears on the screen, she will close her eyes or get up and leave the room. Think about this. Not the real object, but just a picture in a magazine can cause great anxiety and discomfort. And not based on the reality of the situation (like the snake is going to jump out of the T.V. and strangle her), but based on something that has happened to her in the past. Before we chuckle at Mary's behavior, be assured we **all** have "snakes" in our backgrounds that may still be causing us to react irrationally to certain situations.*

4. **Decision.** *This is quite obvious. Based on her quick analysis, Mary makes a reactive decision and says, "That's all folks. I'm out of here," followed by*

primal screams as she runs a 40-yard dash down the aisle, out the building, and probably to the nearest pub.

Now let's see how Sally reacts to the same situation. Sally was raised on a farm. She has been around animals her entire life. She loves animals and do you know what one of her favorite animal is? You've got it, snakes. In fact, Sally has a pet boa constrictor that she endearingly keeps with her in her condo. (A sparse dating life)

So, Sally goes through the same decision making procedure as Mary:

1. *She **perceives** the object through her senses/eyes.*
2. *By **comparison** she identifies the object as a "snake."*
3. *A quick **analysis** stirs up warm and loving feelings.*
4. *She makes a **decision** to move toward the snake, picks it up, caresses it, kisses it, or whatever people do who love snakes.*

Now we get to Jane. She is rather nonplused over this whole situation and is probably wondering why she volunteered to be a participant. She is neither drawn toward snakes nor does she have any fear of them. She remains "inactive" or neutral to the whole situation.

*So in this little example we have three individuals who have three different responses to identically the same situation based not on the reality or truth of the situation, but based on their prior experience(s) or data input regarding the subject. Bottom line, you and I are making decisions based not upon the unlimited potential we all have, but we are making decisions (today) based largely on events or information we have gathered from the past. How often have you sat down and taken inventory of all of your attitudes, opinions, feelings and "facts" and assessed how you might like to think or feel differently about some of these things. The problem is most people don't do this because they don't know **how** to change. They just resign themselves to a self-assessment and internal dialog that says, "I have always been good at _____, I have never been good at _____," and just plod through life acting the same way over and over. It is almost like they are robots whose actions are predetermined by the conscious area of the mind barking out instructions to the subconscious.*

*The subconscious is a servo-mechanism that acts 24/7 on our behalf carrying out the orders given to it by the conscious mind. Let's state again what we just said. Our subconscious is a **servant** that is available to serve us night and day. It is nonjudgmental; it doesn't tell us whether we are making a good* decision or a bad decision. It simply carries out the instructions given to it by its "boss"—the conscious mind. (Remember the captain of the ship and his crew in Chapter 1.)

The subconscious is the greatest tool we have to bring about positive change in any area of our lives, if used properly. We need to better understand the power of our own self talk and take better control of what we request of our subconscious.

This book shows you how to do that.

Before we briefly discuss the supraconscious, let us summarize what we have said. Our present decisions are based largely on our past experiences or information we have about something. We will show you how to modify or change that data which you identify you would like changed. We need to understand that we have also been conditioned to see certain things with a very subjective slant. This is where our prejudices come from.

Once we have been given the tools to bring about positive changes in our lives and we really learn how to use those tools, we are presented with an enormous opportunity to examine our subconscious to determine what data is no longer relevant to our current life experience.

An important thing to understand here is that when we perceive and identify something which strikes a negative habit pattern, the effect knocks out our "Analyzer," and we behave consistent with how we have been conditioned to respond in such a situation. We act **totally** irrationally.

Once we identify our negative habit patterns, we can input new data into our subconscious that will help direct the action we desire. It also rids us of the bind that the negative habit pattern has had on us.

The third area of the mind is the Supraconscious. "Supra" means above or beyond, in this case, consciousness.

Please note that Dr. Murphy does not make reference to the supraconscious. Most of the work in this area of study has been done since Dr. Murphy wrote his book in 1963. The supraconscious is such an important part of our overall being that it must be included in any discussion of truly creative problem solving. In chapter 13, I will outline the step-by-step procedure for accessing this area of our mind.

The supraconscious is our source of all pure creativity. It is in that area where we receive great inspiration and creative solutions, the area where the information needed to solve the situation transcends any data stored in our subconscious, or memory bank. "Geniuses" seem to have an ability to tap into this vast reservoir at will.

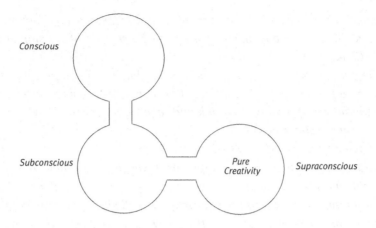

The supraconscious is also our source of motivation and free energy when we are constructively motivated. We will discuss this in detail later as well.

In summary, we have three areas of the mind that all interact with each other—the Conscious, Subconscious, and Supraconscious. However, unless we are aware of them or know how they interact, we are apt to just drift through life on "auto pilot," always doing well in certain areas, poorly in others, and making the same mistakes over and over. But, the promise of this book is, once you fully learn and understand the functions of each of these areas of the mind, combined with the tools we will give you to revise old or outdated information as well as how to input new data to help you achieve your goals more effortlessly, you will truly be able to take control of your life and direct it as you wish. You no longer have to live out a life as a helpless victim.

We create our personal reality through our conscious belief about ourselves, others, and the world . . . We are not at the mercy of the subconscious, or helpless before forces that we cannot understand. The conscious mind directs unconscious activity and has at its command all of the powers of the inner self. These are activated according to our ideas about reality. . . ."

If you do not like your experience, then you must change the nature of your conscious thought and expectations. You must alter the kind of messages that you are sending through your thoughts to your own body, to friends and associates.

The Nature of Personal Reality* by Jane Roberts

And now we move on to the "tools."

*Roberts, op. cit., p. 13

Key 5

AFFIRMATIONS AND VISUALIZATION

Understanding the power in developing mastery in the proper use of Affirmations and Affirmation Techniques.

8

Affirmations and Affirmation Techniques

In Chapter 2, Dr. Murphy introduced the term "auto suggestion" and how people under hypnosis can be given powerful suggestions, which when believed to be true, cause the subject under hypnosis to perform in extraordinary ways. The word "extraordinary" used here is a literal description of the person's behavior when the subconscious picture of what is "ordinary" is temporarily suspended and "ordinary limitations" are replaced with commands and suggestions that cause the hypnotized subject to perform at levels substantially higher than when that person is not under hypnosis.

Most of us have been "hypnotized" by authority figures into believing things about ourselves and their accompanying limitations that are simply not true. But, believing they are true, we act and behave in ways to validate such "truths."

*Hypnotherapist Lee Pulos, Ph.D., has told me that his greatest challenge in working with traumatized adult patients is helping them become **de-hypnotized** to the erroneous data given to them when they were small children and the continuous repetition of such data that led to their traumatized conditions.*

*Let's now examine how the constructive use of affirmations can help reprogram our subconscious with updated, relevant and truthful data that is consistent with who and what we want to be today, not who we used to be! Dr. Murphy stated another term for auto suggestion is **affirmation**.*

Earlier we defined an affirmation as "a statement of fact or belief (positive or negative) that tends to lead you toward the end result you expect." The statement of "fact" or belief may or may not be TRUE, but we believe it to be true and act accordingly. Also, the "end result you expect" may not be the end result you want. But, believing "I have never been good at _____," you resign yourself to that limiting "truth" and program your subconscious with consistent data regarding your limitation so that the subconscious insures your behavior will consistently act in such a way as to support your belief.

You and I have been using affirmations our entire lives. Any statement we make to ourselves or others that follows "I am" or "I" is an affirmation. The following are all affirmations:

- *I am a great spouse.*
- *I am a lousy spouse.*
- *I am a very loving and patient parent.*
- *I always lose my temper around my kids. I guess I'm just not a good parent.*
- *I am very efficient and well organized.*
- *I am sloppy and can never find a thing.*
- *I am a great public speaker.*
- *I always get nervous and screw up when I am in front of a group.*

Remember, we said an affirmation is a statement of fact or belief (positive or negative). In other words, it may not be TRUE (in reality), it is only "true" as we perceive it.

We were not born well organized or poorly organized. We were not born with poor or great public speaking skills. Our attitudes, opinions, and self concept about any of these things (positive or negative) were developed. We were given "factual" data (which may not have been true) at very young ages by authority figures which we interpreted to be true. Over many years these attitudes, opinions, and beliefs were ingrained into us until we believed what we believed, which then became an unalterable "TRUTH" in our personal reality. In fact, the beliefs became so "true" that in extreme cases we were willing to die for them.

Do you realize, for example, that more people have been killed in the history of civilization defending their religious beliefs than any other single or collective cause of death? How can sane people run around the world today killing each other because of differences in their religious beliefs? This is crazy!

*I only use this example to illustrate that affirmations work (positive or negative). We did not genetically come into the world with any thoughts or attitudes about religion, or God, or anything else for that matter. But by having certain doctrines repeated to us over and over, and then with our own self talk repeating them over and over, we shaped, in this example, our religious beliefs **for life** (usually). This was all achieved by the process of affirmations. "I believe _____," "I can _____," and so on. This process also created our self concept.*

So, we know affirmations work.

Therefore, why don't we use this same process to alter our behavior and bring about constructive changes in our lives? In the balance of this chapter, I am going to share with you how to do this.

My first exposure to the formal teachings of affirmation techniques was in 1969 when I attended the Omega Seminar taught by its founder, the late John Boyle (see Introduction).

When I first started using affirmations, I was somewhat skeptical that by simply creating a new sentence to describe how I wanted to be or become, I could achieve such a change. Others attending Omega, who had been through the seminar previously and who had been using affirmations for a period of time, raved about the success they had achieved. There seemed to be no limits to the areas of their lives that were affected (positively) through the deliberate use of affirmations.

Relationships, parenting, health issues, business and financial issues, all seemed to enjoy positive benefits or improvements in the lives of the people giving testimony to their own use of affirmations. I thought if it can work for them, why can't it work for me?

Forty years later I am still using affirmations. This is not to suggest I have not experienced setbacks or failures along the way. But it is to say that the quality of my thinking has been positively affected, which has resulted in a greatly improved quality of how I have chosen to live my life. I once heard, "We teach that which we need to learn the most," and I certainly have lots of room for further growth and development, which I enthusiastically embrace.

Now to the how-to part of writing and using affirmations.

Presuming you have a list of goals or needs you want to achieve, you can now use affirmations as a supplemental technique to assist you in their attainment. Through daily repetition of your affirmations, combined with visualization and strong emotional feelings, you condition or recondition your subconscious to help you achieve your goals.

When you write an affirmation you construct the sentence in first person, present tense, describing the end result you desire as if it were true today.

In other words, you don't say, "My relationship with _____ will get better," or, "My business will improve" (i.e., hope for something better in the future). Rather, you write the affirmation, "I enjoy an excellent relationship with _____ and it gets stronger every day," or, "I am a very successful businessperson and find ways to improve my business each day."

Let's say you want to use affirmations to achieve a health goal. Let's use losing weight as an example. If getting on the scale today reports that your "current reality" is that you weigh 225 pounds and you develop a new goal to weigh 195 pounds, you would develop an affirmation that reads, "I look good and feel good at 195 pounds." This is written in the first person, present tense as though it were true today. You would not write the affirmation, "I am not overweight." The emphasis there is on being overweight, which is exactly the picture you don't want to create.

You may also develop a couple of supportive affirmations such as, "I eat only enough to maintain my perfect weight of 195 pounds," or "I enjoy exercising every day and never miss a day."

Remember, our affirmations are intended to bring about a change in our behavior. The affirmation "I look good and feel good at ___ pounds" does not give us permission to move our bed next to the refrigerator!

It is important that you write an affirmation that lends itself to support visualizations that form the picture of success in your mind that you would like it to be. For example, when you say to yourself, "I enjoy an excellent relationship with _____," you picture yourself and that person together in a setting where you are enjoying each other's company and really having "an excellent relationship." It can be a mental picture from a past experience you enjoyed together or an imaginary picture you simply create to support your affirmation. Either picture (whether actual or imaginary) records in the subconscious mind as though it actually happened provided the picture is supported with strong, positive emotional feelings.

This last step, emotional support, is very important. When people experience age regression hypnosis, for example, they not only recall vividly a visual experience from the past, but they re-experience the emotions associated with that experience. If it was a happy event, they might start laughing whereas a sad event may bring about tears, all under hypnosis. It is important to understand that the purpose of language (words) is to create or access an image. It is this image (not the words) that records in the subconscious along with the feelings and emotions associated with that image. This is why the imagery or picture(s) that support the words, accompanied by feelings and emotions, is so important. We will expand on this in the following chapter.

In summary, the affirmation process consists of three steps:

1. *Read the affirmation to yourself.*
2. *Visually experience a past or future event or an imaginary one that supports your affirmation.*
3. *Inject positive and pleasurable feeling (emotion) into your visualization.*

Each affirmation should last 10–15 seconds and should be repeated three to five times. Like goals, it is usually best to not have more than 15 affirmations at a given time.

Our minds are most receptive to receiving affirmations when we first awake in the morning and at night before we go to bed. I know many people who have their affirmations written on 3 x 5 cards or handheld devices which they keep next to their bed. Jumping ahead for a moment, in Chapter 14 of this book, Dr. Murphy writes:

> You avoid all conflict between your desires and imagination by entering into a drowsy, sleepy state which brings all effort to a minimum. The conscious mind is submerged to a great extent when in a sleepy state. The best time to impregnate your subconscious is prior to sleep. The reason for this is that the highest degree of outcropping of the subconscious occurs prior to sleep and just after we awaken. In this state the negative thoughts and imagery which tend to neutralize your desire and so prevent acceptance by your subconscious mind no longer present themselves. When you imagine the reality of the fulfilled desire and feel the thrill of accomplishment, your subconscious brings about the realization of your desire.

The daily practice of affirmations can bring about almost miraculous changes in one's life. But like anything else, knowing how to do them and doing them are two separate issues. Daily repetition of practicing your affirmations will become a habit. And like all other habits, you will feel "cheated" on the days you don't do them.

I, personally, affirm to do my affirmations daily. I have a written statement which precedes my affirmations which reads:

> *I enjoy reading my affirmations the first thing each morning and the last thing in the evening. My daily practice of affirmations, combined with supportive visualization and strong emotional feelings, imprint into my subconscious mind the values, goals, and attitudes I deem important in the enrichment of my life.*

We have the choice to eliminate negative beliefs. Quoting from The Nature of Personal Reality.*

> Here is a more specific list of . . . beliefs, any of which you may have about yourself.

*Roberts, op. cit., p.13

1. I am sickly, and always have been.
2. There is something wrong with money. People who have it are greedy, less spiritual than those who are poor. They are unhappier and snobs.
3. I am not creative. I have no imagination.
4. I can never do what I want to do.
5. People dislike me.
6. I am fat.
7. I always have bad luck.

These are all beliefs held by many people. Those who have them will meet them in experience. Physical data will always seem to reinforce the beliefs, therefore, but the beliefs formed the reality. . . . you must realize that no one can change your beliefs for you, nor can they be forced upon you from without. You can indeed change them for yourself, however, with knowledge and application.

Hopefully, from your reading thus far you have gained, and will continue to gain, the knowledge and the theory behind 7 KEYS To Unlock Your Full Potential. And from the chapter you have just read, you now have the "applications," i.e., the tools.

Continuing, we will now see the power of directed visualization and the importance of creating and holding in consciousness clearly defined pictures of the end results we desire and expect.

9

Intentionality: The Hidden Power
Within Directed Visualization

As we learned in the previous chapter, "Affirmations and Affirmation Techniques," you:

1. Say the affirmation to yourself in the first-person present tense as though you had already achieved the goal. Examples:

   "I look good and feel good at (goal) pounds."
   "I like (person) unconditionally and enjoy a very good relationship with him/her."

2. Create a visual picture seeing yourself having achieved that goal.
3. Feel the emotion of how good you feel having accomplished this.

Highly effective people have a very clear picture of what they want and where they are going. Their pictures are **laser** sharp. If it's a better home, they have a clear picture of what that home looks like: The number of bedrooms, one story or two, pool, choice of neighborhoods, price range, etc., etc. Those who often fall short of their goals lack the intensity of a clearly defined picture of what the accomplishment of that goal may look like. The affirmation, "I want a better home" unsupported by the clarity of what that home looks like dissipates the energy required to bring the goal to fruition.

As a small boy, I use to take a magnifying glass on a hot summer day and hold it steady over a piece of paper that would suddenly erupt in flames. What is interesting is that if I held the magnifying glass up to the sun and just passed it aimlessly over my arm (wandering), I wouldn't feel a thing, not even a small amount of heat. But, if I focused it on, say, a freckle on my arm, within a matter of seconds I would quickly move the magnifying glass or suffer a severe burn. Why?

Think about this. The source of the energy, the sun, is constant. But the magnifying glass when properly focused, harnesses that energy and magnifies *its power manyfold. The same thing happens when we are* crystal clear *on what we want and continue to relentlessly hold that thought (picture) and the emotional intensity associated with that picture. We then both harness and magnify the power of the subconscious to manifest this picture and bring it into reality in our lives. In Chapter 13, "The Supraconscious and Creative Problem Solving," we will learn the* basic operating principle *that states, "Any thought held on a continuous basis in the conscious mind must be brought into reality by the supraconscious mind (positive or negative)."*

As we proceed through this chapter, we will provide specific *examples of how this happens.*

The important thing to remember here is that what records in our subconscious mind is not the words that we impart, but rather the pictures (images) the words create and *the emotions associated with those images. This has now been proven scientifically by Montreal neurologist Dr. Wilder Penfield. Dr. Penfield would take a person and put him under a local anaesthetic. The person is awake. Dr. Penfield then removes a portion of the skull over the area of the brain that stores memory. He probes into the brain and the subject recites an earlier experience in their life as though it is actually happening* NOW! *If it is a happy event, the subject is smiling and laughing. If it is a sad event, the subject is despondent and crying. If Dr. Penfield removes the probe and inserts it in exactly the same place, the subject will express the same subjective experience. It is as though someone punched the rewind button on a recorder.*

As we have learned in Chapter 7, everything we have experienced in life and the images and *emotions associated with those experiences are all stored in the subconscious area of our mind and effect our current behavior.*

The following is further scientific evidence of how visualization can effect performance.

Dr. Alvaro Pascual-Leone is Professor of Neurology at Beth Israel Deaconess Medical Center at Harvard Medical School.

Referring again to Dr. Doidge's book, The Brain That Changes Itself, *Dr. Doidge writes how Dr. Pascual-Leone has transcended the technology developed by Penfield through the process of transcranial magnetic stimulations, or TMS. As Dr. Doidge writes,*

> Wilder Penfield had to open the skull surgically and insert his electric probe into the brain to stimulate the motor or sensory cortex. When Pascual-Leone turns on the machine (TMS) and makes my finger move, I experience *exactly* what Penfield's pa-

tients did when he cut open their skull and prodded them with large electrodes.

Dr. Pascual-Leone had great success in accelerating the learning of Braille by blind people using his TMS techniques.

Dr. Doidge continues to discuss Pascual-Leone's success in proving the power and relationship of directed visualization and performance:

His next venture would break ground in a new way altogether, by showing that our thoughts can change the material structure of our brains.

He would study the way thoughts change the brain by using TMS to observe changes in the finger maps of people learning to play the piano. One of Pascual-Leone's heroes, the great Spanish neuro-anatomist and Nobel Laureate, Santiago Ranon y Cajal, who spent his later life looking in vain for brain plasticity, proposed in 1894 that the organ of thoughts is, within certain limits, malleable, and perfectible by well-directed mental exercises. In 1904 he argued that thoughts, repeated in "mental practice," must strengthen the existing neuronal connections and create new ones. He also had the intuition that this process would be particularly pronounced in neurons that control the fingers in pianists, who do so much mental practice.

Ranon y Cajal, using his imagination, had painted a picture of a plastic brain but lacked the tools to prove it. Pascual-Leone now thought he had a tool in TMS to test whether mental practice and imagination in fact lead to physical changes.

The details of the imagining experiment were simple and picked up Cajal's idea to use the piano. Pascual-Leone taught two groups of people, who had *never* studied piano, a sequence of notes, showing them which fingers to move and letting them hear the notes as they were played. Then members of one group, the "mental practice" group, sat in front of an electric piano keyboard, two hours a day, for five days, and *imagined* both playing the sequence and hearing it played. A second "physical practice" group actually played the music two hours a day for five days. Both groups had their brains mapped before the experiment, each day during it, and afterward. Then both groups were asked to play the sequence, and a computer measured the accuracy of their performances.

Pasqual-Leone found that both groups learned to play the sequence, and both showed similar brain map changes. Remarkably, mental practice alone produced the same physical changes in the motor system as actually playing the piece. By the end of the fifth day, the changes in motor signals to the muscles were the same in both groups, and the imaging players were as accurate as the actual players were on their third day.

The level of improvement at five days in the mental practice group, however, substantially was not as great as in those who did physical practice. But, when the mental practice group finished its mental training and was given a single two-hour physical practice session, its overall performance improved to the level of the physical practice group's performance at five days. Clearly mental practice is an effective way to prepare for learning a physical skill with minimal physical practice."

Dr. Doidge continues,

One of the most advanced forms of mental practice is "mental chess," played without a board or pieces. The players imagine the board and the play, keeping track of the positions. Anatoly Sharansky, the Soviet human rights activist, used mental chess to survive in prison. Sharansky, a Jewish computer specialist falsely accused of spying for the United States in 1977, spent nine years in prison, four hundred days of that time in solitary confinement in freezing, darkened, five-by-six-foot punishment cells. Political prisoners in isolation often fall apart mentally because the use-it-or-lose-it brain needs external stimulation to maintain its maps. During this extended period of sensory deprivation, Sharansky played mental chess for months on end, which probably helped him keep his brain from degrading. He played both white and black, holding the game in his head, from opposite perspectives— an extraordinary challenge to the brain. Sharansky once told me, half joking, that he kept at chess thinking he might as well use the opportunity to become the world champion. After he was released, with the help of Western pressure, he went to Israel and became a Cabinet minister. When the World Champion, Garry Kasparov, played against the prime minister and leader of the Cabinet, he beat all of them except Sharansky.

. . . One reason we can change our brains simply by imagining is that, from a neuroscientific point of view, imagining an act and doing it are not as different as they seem. When people close their eyes and visualize a simple object, such as the letter "A," the primary visual cortex lights up, just as it would if the subject were actually looking at the letter "A." Brain scans show that in action and imagination many of the same parts of the brain are activated. That is why visualizing can improve performance.

Thank you, Dr. Doidge.

Now let me share with you an actual life experience that further documents the power of directed visualization.

In 1975, while flying home to Portland, Oregon, from Los Angeles, I read The Inner Game of Tennis *by W. Timothy Gallwey. I was so impressed with Tim's writing that I tracked him down and invited him to come to Portland to talk with our company's management team as well as the Oregon chapter of the Young Presidents' Organization.*

As a result of that encounter, Tim and I developed a friendship and association, and to this day I consider him one of the greatest mentors/teachers in my life. He really taught me the inner game of performance in any area of my life for which he simply used tennis as a metaphor for such teachings and insights.

In 1976 Tim invited my wife, Jeri, and me to join him and a group at Copper Mountain, Colorado. With co-author Bob Kriegel, the Copper Mountain ski experience was to become the basis for Tim's next book, Inner Skiing.

My wife and I have both been skiing since early childhood. I was on our high school ski team and raced competitively in pro-amateur events until the age of 50. Even as I write these words, my wife and I are enjoying the month skiing in Sun Valley, Idaho. My point being that I am not a stranger to skiing or conventional ski instruction.

Approximately 30 of us gathered together at Copper Mountain to experience a week of "inner skiing." As those of you who are skiers know, conventional ski instruction is very linear where the instructor observes you for a couple of ski turns and then says, "bend zee knees," or "put more weight on the downhill ski," etc., etc. The whole process is very mechanical.

None of this occurred at Copper Mountain, and yet our skiing proficiency increased dramatically. We began each day by grouping together after breakfast in one of the hotel's ballrooms where we were staying. We were in our ski attire and were invited to lie down on the carpet of the ballroom. We experienced a group deep relaxation exercise and then with our eyes closed we were asked to visualize ourselves skiing. We were given several differ-

*Doige, o.p. cit., p. 31

ent *visual scenarios such as different terrains, moguls, smooth slopes, steep slopes and gentle slopes. In each scenario we were instructed to visualize ourselves skiing in that situation. We did this exercise for 30–45 minutes. We then adjourned and gathered with our respective groups, put on our skis and hit the slopes.*

Once on the mountain, our instructor (really more a facilitator) would tell us he was going to go down the mountain making 10–15 turns, and then we were to follow and ski to him, one at a time. As each of us arrived, he only asked one question; "How was that compared to your visualization this morning?" The skier would respond, "I think I was bent over too far at the waist," or, "I was using too much upper body movement," etc. The instructor would simply say, "Good, just become more aware of your picture this morning."

There was no agreeing or disagreeing with our own assessment. There was no correctional instruction—simply, "be aware of your mental picture this morning."

Note: Very Important:

When you internally visualize yourself performing, you don't see yourself making mistakes. In skiing you don't visualize yourself falling, you see yourself skiing flawlessly. If you are visualizing your golf swing, you don't see yourself hitting the ball out of bounds, you see yourself hitting the ball down the center of the fairway or hitting the ball on the green next to the pin. If you are visualizing yourself playing the piano, you don't see yourself hitting the wrong keys. You see yourself playing the piece perfectly.

This is a very important fact associated with visualizing performance, as it becomes the subconscious recorded picture and instruction to your subconscious of how you are to perform.

As we skied our next 10–15 turns, once again the instructor would ask, "How was that?" We might answer by saying, "I wasn't as bent over at the waist and my upper body movement was more centered." The instructor wouldn't say, "good" or" bad," he would simply say, "Great, just continue to focus on your image during our visualization this morning."

Throughout the day and the week our performance continued to improve with no instruction. We were our own "instructors."

One very impressive exercise occurred one day when we stood at the top of a Double Diamond run. These are the most difficult and challenging of all the ski runs on the mountain. Our instructor completely unbuckled his boots and then asked each of us to do the same. He said, "When I get to the bottom, each of you ski down to me one at a time." He then took off skiing the terrain masterfully and when he got to the bottom of the hill, he came to a sudden stop, planted his poles in the snow, and leapt completely out of his boots landing softly with his stocking feet in the snow. We were all flabbergasted.

When it came my turn to ski the run, I pushed off from the top, made a few awkward turns, and heard my inner voice screaming, "I'm going to kill myself!" At another level, however, I was aware that our whole week was about turning off that voice of fear and doubt (what Tim calls Self One) and trusting that my inner self (Self Two) knows exactly what to do, if we can keep Self One out of the way.

So, I gently told Self One to "shut up!!" and I surrendered to the trust that Self Two would know perfectly what to do. I skied the rest of that run as well as I have ever skied an expert run, and with my boots completely unbuckled, which is the complete antithesis of any conventional teachings or instruction.

Self One is always clamoring for attention and is the little voice that loves to judge everything. By becoming aware of how distractive and destructive Self One can be, when he now comes knocking on my door, I gently (not too) tell him to "buzz off" and re-center myself in the present.

Whatever you clearly visualize and imprint into your subconscious mind, you will actualize into your present reality.

As I am finishing these thoughts, I am watching the 2010 Winter Olympics at Whistler, British Columbia. Visa keeps showing an advertisement where alpine skier medalist, Julia Mancuso, drew a picture of herself when she was nine years old. The picture was of Julia winning the Gold Medal in women's skiing. From the time she was nine years old, she looked at that picture almost every day. In the 2006 Winter Olympics at the age of 21, Julia Mancuso won the Gold Medal.

Need we say more?!

The bottom line is we are what we visualize, think, and believe.

10

Building Personal Power

by Lee Pulos, Ph.D., ABPP

In the Foreword to this book, Lee Pulos, Ph.D., clinical psychologist, writes,

Of the thousands of patients I have seen over the years for a variety of issues, I would estimate that at least 95 percent of them had an issue with self-esteem, a sense of worthiness or unworthiness, which can influence the inner sense of deservability for love, success, health, or prosperity.

Because of the importance of self esteem and its relationship to this overall book, I asked Lee if he would please write the chapter on this subject.

Lee writes:

Self-esteem is the immune system of the mind and of the spirit. Self-esteem is our experience of feeling competent to cope with the basic challenges of life and feeling happy and worthy and deserving of happiness. People who have the greatest sense of self-esteem are those who feel they are doing their life's work. Genuine self-esteem is still feeling good about ourselves when things are *not* going right.

Self respect has to do with our value as a person; an inner certainty, a sense of happiness, a feeling of success about life and feeling worthy enough to attract, allow, and receive love into our life. People with a lesser sense of self-estimate, or esteem, find it easier to give love than to receive it.

If you have a healthy immune system, does that mean you will never get sick? Of course not. But you will be less susceptible to illness, and you will experience a faster recovery. Having a high level of self-esteem doesn't mean you will never be anxious, miserable, depressed, or over-whelmed on occasion. The advantages of having a strong sense of self and worthiness is that you have good psychological shock absorbers. If you are attempting to achieve a goal and hit a wall, you will persevere. You may not always succeed, but you will succeed more often than you fail. A top manager in one of the executive seminars I was conducting said to the group, "I have been knocked down five times—but I got up six." The average CEO has had 3.2 major failures before succeeding.

Persons with a low sense of self-esteem will go through the motions of persevering but will fail more often than they succeed. Our self-esteem generates a certain level of expectancy and expectancies become self-ful-filling prophecies.

While our sense of self-esteem shows up in different areas of our life, it shows up most prominently and consistently in the area of relationships and love. If a person doesn't feel they are lovable, they will find it hard to believe someone else loves them and will usually find ways to sabotage the relation-ship in some fashion. Have you ever tried to tell or convey love to a person who doesn't feel lovable? There isn't much you can do to convince them.

Our self-esteem, of course, will vary in different areas of our lives and our effectiveness level, performance, or success will correspond to our self-esteem in that particular area. For example, you may have high self-esteem as a manager and communicator of ideas, and your perfor-mance or effectiveness level will correspond to your own self-estimate. You may have low self-esteem with mechanical things or replacing parts and putting gadgets together. You and your friends may lovingly call you a "klutz" in that area. You may have average self-esteem as a parent or spouse, and your competence in that area will correspond accordingly.

If you take all the areas of your life and make a bar graph of high and low effectiveness levels, you will probably end up with a zigzag profile. Psychologists would average that out and come up with what is called a "g" factor, or general level of self-esteem.

Utilizing certain exercises to change limiting beliefs in specific areas of your life and, of course, re-educating and re-programming your sub-conscious with affirmations, visualizations and/or self-hypnosis will also work in improving your effectiveness level in these different areas.

Thus, self-esteem is the reputation we acquire with ourselves. Our self-concept is broader than self-esteem and is the umbrella, so to speak, which subsumes our beliefs, ideals, and our body image, which is an important part of our self concept. It includes our liabilities, assets, limitations, and capabilities; self-esteem is one of its major components.

The importance of self-esteem was first drawn to national attention over forty years ago following the publication of *Psycho-Cybernetics** by cosmetic surgeon, Dr. Maxwell Maltz. In his book he described how he would volunteer one morning a week to do cosmetic surgery on prison inmates in the local penitentiary. After two years or so the warden called Dr. Maltz into his office and pointed out that the men whose nose jobs and facial disfigurements that were improved through plastic surgery were not committing more crimes and returning to jail following their release from prison. Dr. Maltz realized by changing their body image, which, as I noted earlier, is a very important part of self-image, the convicts felt better about themselves. He went on to describe self-esteem as "the most important discovery of the 20th century." However, this is not necessarily true of everyone.

In later writings, Dr. Maltz described two female patients who had radical cosmetic surgery on their faces. In assessing themselves after the bandages were removed and the swelling disappeared, both women looked and looked at themselves and very sadly and disapprovingly said, "I don't look any different. Not much has changed. I still feel the same about myself." That was when Dr. Maltz realized that self-image, for most people, was internal and not the external trappings of what we call beauty.

Along the same lines I remember an almost painfully candid interview during which Elizabeth Taylor described herself as "short, pudgy, awful thighs. I hate my nose, my eyes are too far apart, and I don't like the shape of my face. I wish I could change my whole appearance at times." That self-description from one of the most beautiful women in the world. No wonder she had such a series of self-destructive behaviors: eating binges, drug and alcohol abuse, a number of accidents and multiple surgeries, eight marriages and so on. Self-esteem is an inside job.

* *Maltz, Maxwell. Psycho-Cybernetics,* A New Way to Get More Living Out of Life. *Pocket. 1989.*

What I would like to segue into now is to describe some of the qualities of low self-esteem. As we become aware of certain qualities, with awareness comes the potential for change, the opportunity to begin scraping off some of the psychological barnacles that we all have, to varying degrees, on our cruise ship of life.

The first quality is that of *victimhood*. Victims have little or no confidence in themselves. They feel sorry for themselves, and feel they have been wronged in life. They also feel unappreciated, misunderstood and treated unfairly. Victims rarely want to be responsible for anything. They will try to get you to do things for them. Victims frequently try to manipulate people through guilt to try to get people to be their rescuers. But they will never be able to do enough for them. They always feel let down so they can blame other people or circumstances for their failings.

Victims give their power to the past: "If I had different parents, if my dad had more money . . .," blame, blame, blame, which is a cheap hit of power, the only power they have since they give it away.

A brief sidebar here. Some people may feel that low self-esteem is found mostly in people on the lower rungs of the ladder of life. Two years ago I had a new patient walk into my office dressed all in black leather, chains, and an angry, mean expression on her face. As I took her history she told me she was a Dominatrix. I gulped. She went on to say that men pay her good money to abuse and insult them and do demeaning things in her apartment. She assured me there was nothing of a sexual nature in her work. I wondered out loud, what kind of men would subject themselves to such humiliating behavior. She said that one of her clients was a supreme court judge, two were successful business men, and one was a lawyer. That shocked me. She went on to say that these men suffered from the Impostor Syndrome. They had gotten to the top of their profession or vocation but didn't feel they belonged there, and to use her words, "They have low self-esteem and they come to me so I can cut them down to size to where they feel they belong." It was quite an eye-opener for me and another day in my office where my patient became my teacher.

Let us move on to the second quality of low self-esteem, which is *Martyrhood*. Our culture, the Judeo-Christian ethic that so many of us have been conditioned to and raised by, emphasizes the virtues of learning through pain. "No pain, no gain." Our culture has also revered struggle and suffering, and every major religious teacher is exemplified by their virtue of struggle, hardship, and sacrifice. This has been conditioned into our collective, or consensus, consciousness so that some people don't feel right about achieving or succeeding without first going through struggle, hurt, mini-failures. and so on. But let us look more clearly at some of the qualities of martyrhood so we can identify them and if they apply to us, then do what we can to eliminate them.

The first quality of martyrhood is feeling *unappreciated*, i.e., "Nobody knows the trouble I know, nobody works as hard as me, you don't appreciate the difficulties and obstacles I have to overcome," and so on.

Martyrs almost always feel they are being mistreated or misjudged. They have a sense of hopelessness and almost always feel misunderstood.

Another quality of low personal power or self-esteem is around the feeling of *undeservability,* which can hold you back and stagnate you in the past. Undeservability also puts future successes out of reach and more or less slows your momentum into the future. It freezes you in the past or takes you back to where you were rather than where you are going.

It is important that you silently introspect and look at this very crucial issue of deservability since it has been demonstrated time and time again to hold people back and lower their sense of worth, initiative and drive. Time and time again, while taking history in my office, I hear the words, "I don't deserve. . .," "I am not worthy of . . ." whatever the issue—and these are often well educated persons with good jobs and families.

The next quality of low self worth and esteem is *shame.* No emotion wounds as deeply as shame. It is at the root of many human conflicts. People who have been treated with ridicule, contempt, disdain, betrayal, abuse or abandonment, or received excessive punishment as children experience an almost continuous low-grade sense of humiliation and unworthiness. Also, children and adults who have never been appreciated or shown empathy and understanding end up almost apologizing for their existence. The depth of the shame should determine whether this issue is best dealt with professional help.

Because of strong feelings of self-doubt and self-mistrust, people who are metaphorically on "shaky stilts" frequently apologize for themselves or for their opinions or even for their existence, and will bend over backward to please in order to avoid any kind of rejection. Along the same line, people with a low estimate of themselves are fearful of change. They have a very narrow range in their comfort zone and will rarely make changes and step outside the box to challenge or confront a person whose ideas they may not agree with.

Because of their inner insecurities, like attracts like. People with low esteem levels usually end up with each other. You will rarely see a person with high self-esteem be in a partnership with or marry someone who doesn't value themselves. Relationships and marriages sometimes break up because one of the partners decides to be "more than." He or she will take courses, read books, and attend seminars. As they grow and develop more emotional muscle and inner strength, they sadly discover that they have little in common with their partner, who chooses to stay inside their narrow but safe comfort zone. Often, they move on.

As mentioned earlier, people with low self-esteem seek a sense of self-worth through trying to be popular and by being people-pleasers. They will acquire lots of toys and material acquisitions and will try to improve their worth with cosmetic surgery or sexual exploits and conquests. These do make us feel better, temporarily, and changing a part of one's body image can contribute to a higher sense of worth. But again, self-esteem is best changed from the inside out, not the other way around.

I believe that everyone in the world has some issues, doubts, or questions about their inner confidence and self-esteem. The whole point of sharing what we have covered so far is to do an inventory of what *you* would like to change, stop doing, or read up on so that you can begin building and increasing your psychological net worth! Remember, even more important than our beliefs, which are the building blocks for our way of being in the world, is *Choice!* We can choose to remain in the status quo or our comfort zone, or to experience the discomfort of change and create a different trajectory of our life. Obviously, by choosing to read this book, you have made a choice to release some of the old and to start breathing life into the new.

Just a brief reminder of how the 70,000 or so active receptors on our cells are tuned in to certain frequencies or signals. Some are tuned to our external environment, but many of the receptors have been programmed to the resonance and frequency of our attitudes and beliefs. As we stop the mental frequency of say, struggle and martyrhood, those receptors will stop triggering the release of stress hormones. As we begin breathing life into new ways of being in the world, whether more loving, more forgiving, or less judgmental, other receptors will respond to the new frequencies, the more empowering resonances, and will trigger the release of healing and feel-good molecules, which in turn will contribute to a greater sense of confidence to take the risk of making desired changes in our lives.

Let us now move on and look at some of the qualities that people with high self-esteem share to varying degrees.

The *first* quality is that they are continually seeking the challenge and stimulation of worthwhile *goals*. Goals, of course, are the purpose to all human activity. It is not necessary or even possible to achieve all of our goals, but to help us become more than what we were. Goals are like dreams and many people, rather than dreaming their own future, allow themselves to be woven into other people's dreams. There are two ways to create our reality: to set goals and program an optimal future or simply allow whatever comes our way. Both are programs. Both work. High self-esteem people love themselves enough to dream, to create the optimal future they will be stepping into.

High self-esteem people realize that material things such as a fancy car or a mountain condo are symptoms of success, but not true success. True success is intrinsic in the way you treat yourself, your family, and other people.

People with a strong sense of self-worth **live consciously** as problem-solvers having a respect for facts, for truths, for being present in the now when someone is talking to them. They have a passion for self-awareness, for honest self-examination and an awareness of their inner world, not just the external world. And they don't anaesthetize themselves with denial or addictions such as drugs or alcohol.

Most important, they are quick to forgive themselves and others. They release the past and don't try to make the present conform to the past by hanging on to grudges or seeking revenge. They realize that it is not the prisoners who spend the most time in prison, it's the warden. If you are keeping someone as an emotional hostage, then you are the prisoner. All healing, as mentioned earlier, has to go through the door of forgiveness.

Another quality is that people who value themselves value others and treat them with respect. You will never hear racist, sexist, or ageist remarks from people who feel good about themselves. They go out of their way to honor, respect and ennoble people regardless of sexual orientation, race, religious beliefs, or age.

As indicated earlier, high self-esteemers form *nourishing* rather than toxic *relationships*. They have open, honest communication skills and look for clarity rather than fearing it. If giving feedback, they take responsibility for their feelings and instead of a "you" blaming remark, will preface a statement with "I feel this way for what just happened."

Another component is *humility*. That doesn't mean false modesty or apologizing for being who you are. But regardless of how many times you have experienced a person in a certain way say, for example, if they are a gossip, or bossy, then humility is being open to each moment in life as something new by not prejudging that so and so is a bore. Rather, it's having the humility to let that person be different this time. Humility is seeing each moment or experience as brand new without judgment.

Altruism is an additional quality of high self-esteem. Altruism, or being helpful or of service to others whether by doing volunteer work, being a big brother/big sister, or whatever one chooses to contribute to create a higher sense of well-being or even excitement. Women in one social helping program reported that by volunteering for service at a convalescent home for older folks, they felt a long-lasting sense of deep inner satisfaction, even exhilaration, and an increased sense of self-worth, less depression and fewer aches and pains.

People with a higher sense of self-esteem also have a higher sense of accountability. Let me give you an example. One of my friends called me not too long ago, offered to buy me lunch and wanted to talk about how devastated he was as his wife had run off with his best friend. I thought, "Oh no, he wants to get into blame and self-pity." So much for my humility in this instance. Instead, despite his torment he said, "Lee, you have known me for a long time, and you have been with my wife and me on many occasions. What was it about me, what could I have done or didn't do that caused her to leave me?" I was almost in tears, as I could feel his pain yet he wanted to take accountability for what had happened rather than give his power away to blaming or "poor me's." In other words, he acknowledged that he is accountable for creating his life and his reality, and that whatever he did or didn't do led to a very sad chapter in his life. But also he ended up, over time, learning a great deal more about himself.

People with a higher sense of self-esteem are also opening up more to an *emerging spirituality,* to a sense of connectedness to all living things, creatures and humans alike, to realizing that there is a higher power and how can one increase their connectedness to this creative energy. There is also a greater appreciation of mother earth and the environment and how can I be more loving, more giving to others. Spirituality, of course, has different meanings for different people, and I am sure you will find a way of interpreting this for yourself.

Finally, high self-esteem people will argue for their magnificence and the magnificence of other people rather than for their limitations.

But, what can we do on a conscious level without years of psychotherapy or psychological excavations to strengthen our inner strong self? Can all of the above be distilled and simplified? Following are the four qualities of self-esteem that I share with all my patients since they can be managed and controlled consciously.

High self-esteem people have good boundaries. They can draw that line in the sand and say "no" to what doesn't fit or seem right to them. In other words, they choose to define themselves, their needs and beliefs rather than giving their power away and allowing others to define them.

Secondly, and perhaps most important, they avoid all judgments. Discernment, yes, but whenever you judge someone else, you are judging a part of yourself in them that you don't approve of in yourself. Judgments freeze a part of you in the past and blind you to your real self. Thus, all judgments implicitly are self-judgments. Learning to love yourself and learning to love others go hand in hand.

Thirdly, as mentioned previously, our inner dialogue or self talk carries on throughout our waking hours at 150–300 words per minute or 45,000 to 50,000 thoughts per day! Since all thoughts are treated like "prayers" by the subconscious (it does not judge), what are you "praying" for all day long? High self-esteem people carefully monitor their inner dialogue as to whether they are "drugging" their minds all day long with good hypnosis or bad hypnotic thoughts. Are we planting weeds or flowers in the garden of our subconscious?

And fourthly, high self-esteem people feel worthy of both receiving from and giving to others. Generally, people with a low self-estimate will be "pleasers" and over-accommodating so as to not risk being rejected by expressing their own needs. In some instances, the only way pleasers can justify receiving is to subconsciously get "sick" or have an accident, which makes it acceptable to be nurtured or taken care of.

Fortunately, all of the above can be controlled consciously with mindfulness, giving from the heart, and embracing one's self and others without judgment.

Negative and self-limiting thoughts are the real enemy we must face. They diminish our spirit, our mind, our sense of self-hood and the way we estimate ourselves—our self-esteem.

People often ask me, "Is all this concern about self-esteem something recent that has come about with the New Age movement?" Over 2,000 years ago one of the greatest teachers of all time said, "Love thy neighbor as thyself." You cannot love thy neighbor if you don't love yourself. You cannot give away what you don't have.

That completes the invaluable contribution of my colleague Lee Pulos. Thanks so much for this wonderful input, Lee.

People with high self esteem consciously work at it. They understand these principles as well as applying the tools outlined in this book to build high self esteem.

Two excellent affirmations for the building of high self esteem are:

"I like (love) myself unconditionally."
"I never devalue myself (or others) with destructive criticism."

11

Mental Healings in Modern Times

Over the past four decades, the Institute of Noetic Sciences (IONS) has had a catalytic influence on the evolution of mainstream medicine and the frontiers of scientific inquiry. Our investigation into the role of consciousness in healing has significantly contributed to the scientific understanding of how the mind influences health. Our work helped to transform mind-body medicine from a fringe idea into a vital component of virtually all major medical centers in the United States and, increasingly, worldwide. Our original research on the benefits of meditation and compassion sparked the development of new scientific methods and insights into how we can cultivate our highest potentials. Our pioneering scientific work on interconnectedness through time and space has challenged traditional notions of the nature of reality and is now making its way into mainstream physics. Our frontier research into perennial mysteries, including precognition, life after death, prayer and healing, and transformative experiences, continues to broaden the range of acceptable topics for scientific inquiry. In short, IONS continues to expand the boundaries of our understanding of ourselves and of reality.

—Marilyn Mandala Schlitz, Ph.D.
President/CEO
Institute of Noetic Sciences

We have been reading about the mind and consciousness. There continues to be a growing body of scientific evidence supporting the mind's role in facilitating the healing of the physical body. Please enjoy Dr. Murphy's chapter, "Mental Healings in Modern Times." At the conclusion of this chapter, I will share with you a personal healing experience I had in 1981 that fully supports Dr. Murphy's teaching.

Everyone is definitely concerned with the healing of bodily conditions and human affairs. What is it that heals? Where is this healing power?

These are questions asked by everyone. The answer is that this healing power is in the subconscious mind of each person, and a changed mental attitude on the part of the sick person releases this healing power.

No mental or religious science practitioner, psychologist, psychiatrist, or medical doctor ever healed a patient. The psychologist or psychiatrist proceeds to remove the mental blocks in the patient so that the healing principle may be released, restoring the patient to health. Likewise, the surgeon removes the physical block enabling the healing currents to function as normal. No physician, surgeon, or mental-science practitioner claims that he "healed the patient." The one healing power is called by many names— Nature, Life, God, Creative Intelligence, and Subconscious Power.

There are many different methods used to remove the mental, emotional, and physical blocks which inhibit the flow of the healing life principle animating all of us. The healing principle resident in your subconscious mind can and will, if properly directed by you or some other person, heal your mind and body of all disease. Your subconscious will heal the burn or cut on your hand even though you may profess to be an atheist or agnostic.

The modern mental therapeutic procedure is based on the truth that the infinite intelligence and power of your subconscious mind responds according to your beliefs. The mental science practitioner goes into his closet and shuts the door, which means he stills his mind, relaxes, lets go, and thinks of the infinite healing presence within him. He closes the door of his mind to all outside distractions as well as appearances, and then quietly and knowingly turns over his request or desire to his subconscious mind, realizing that the intelligence of his mind will answer him according to his specific needs.

The most wonderful thing to know is this: Imagine the end desired and feel its reality; then the infinite life principle will respond to your conscious choice and your conscious request. This is the meaning of believe you have received, and you shall receive. This is what the modern mental scientist does when he practices healing therapy.

One process of healing

There is only one universal healing principle operating through everything—the cat, the dog, the tree, the grass, the wind, the earth—for everything is alive. This life principle operates through the animal, vegetable, and mineral kingdoms as instinct and the law of growth. Man is consciously aware of this life principle, and he can consciously direct it to bless himself in countless ways.

There are many different approaches, techniques, and methods in using the universal power, but there is only one process of healing, which is faith and belief.

The law of belief

All religions of the world represent forms of belief, and these beliefs are explained in many ways. The law of life is belief. What do you believe about yourself, life, and the universe?

Belief is a thought in your mind which causes the power of your subconscious to be distributed into all phases of your life according to your thinking habits. The belief of your mind is simply the thought of your mind.

It is foolish to believe in something to hurt or harm you. Remember, it is not the thing believed in that hurts or harms you, but the belief or thought in your mind which creates the result. All your experiences, all your actions, and all the events and circumstances of your life are but the reflections and reactions to your own thought.

Affirmations and directed visualization are the combined function of the conscious and subconscious mind scientifically directed.

Affirmations are the synchronized, harmonious, and intelligent function of the conscious and subconscious levels of mind specifically directed for a definite purpose. In scientific prayer or affirmations, you must know what you are doing and why you are doing it. You trust the law of healing. Affirmations are sometimes referred to as mental treatment, and another term is scientific prayer.

In the affirmation process, you consciously choose a certain idea, mental picture, or plan which you desire to experience. You realize your capacity to convey this idea or mental image to your subconscious by feeling the reality of the state assumed. As you remain faithful in your mental attitude, your affirmation will be answered. The affirmation process is a definite mental action for a definite specific purpose. (See Chapter 8).

Let us suppose that you decide to heal a certain difficulty by using the affirmation process. You are aware that your problem or sickness, whatever it may be, must be caused by negative thoughts charged with fear and lodged in your subconscious mind. And that if you can succeed in cleansing your mind of these thoughts, you will get a healing.

You therefore turn to the healing power within your own subconscious mind and remind yourself of its infinite power and intelligence and its capacity to heal all conditions. As you dwell on these truths, your fear will begin to dissolve, and the recollection of these truths also corrects the erroneous beliefs.

You give thanks for the healing that you know will come, and then you keep your mind off the difficulty until you feel guided, after an interval, to affirm again. While you are affirming, you absolutely refuse to give any power to the negative conditions or to admit for a second that the healing will not come. This attitude of mind brings about the harmonious union of the conscious and subconscious mind, which releases the healing power.

Faith healing, what it means, and how blind faith works

What is popularly termed faith healing is not the faith mentioned in the Bible, which means a knowledge of the interaction of the conscious and subconscious mind. A faith healer is one who heals without any real scientific understanding of the powers and forces involved. He may claim that he has a special gift of healing, and the sick person's blind belief in him or his powers may bring results.

A voodoo doctor in South Africa and other parts of the world may heal by incantations, or a person may be healed by touching the so-called bones of saints, or anything else which causes the patients to honestly believe in the method or process.

Any method which causes you to move from fear and worry to faith and expectancy will heal. There are many persons, each of whom claims that because his personal theory produces results, it is, therefore, the correct one. This, as already explained in this chapter, cannot be true.

To illustrate how blind faith works: The Viennese physician, Franz Anton Mesmer, in 1776 claimed many cures when he stroked diseased bodies with artificial magnets. Later on he threw away his magnets and evolved the theory of animal magnetism. This he held to be a fluid which pervades the universe, but is most active in the human organism.

He claimed that this magnetic fluid, which was going forth from him to his patients, healed them. People flocked to him, and many wonderful cures were effected.

Mesmer moved to Paris, and while there the Government appointed a commission composed of physicians and members of the Academy of Science, of which Benjamin Franklin was a member, to investigate his cures. The report admitted the leading facts claimed by Mesmer, but held that there was no evidence to prove the correctness of his magnetic fluid theory, and said the effects were due to the imagination of the patients.

Soon after this, Mesmer was driven into exile, and died in 1815. Shortly afterwards, Dr. Braid of Manchester undertook to show that magnetic fluid had nothing to do with the production of the healings of Dr. Mesmer. Dr. Braid discovered that patients could be thrown into hypnotic sleep by focusing their attention on the flame of a candle during which many of the many of the well-known phenomena ascribed to magnetism by Mesmer could be produced. Braid called hypnosis "the physiology of fascination" (*fascination,* here, has the sense of *absorption*).

You can readily see that all these cures were undoubtedly brought about by the active imagination of the patients together with a powerful suggestion of health to their subconscious minds. All this could be termed blind faith as there was no understanding in those days as to how the cures were brought about.

Releasing the kinetic action of the subconscious mind

A psychologist friend of mine told me that one of his lungs was infected. X-rays and analysis showed the presence of tuberculosis. At night before going to sleep he would quietly affirm, "Every cell, nerve, tissue, and muscle of my lungs are now being made whole, pure, and perfect. My whole body is being restored to health and harmony."

These are not his exact words, but they represent the essence of what he affirmed. A complete healing followed in about a month's time. Subsequent X-rays showed a perfect healing.

I wanted to know his method, so I asked him why he repeated the words prior to sleep. Here is his reply, "The kinetic action of the subconscious mind continues throughout your sleep-time period. Hence, give the subconscious mind something good to work on as you drop off into slumber." This was a very wise answer. In thinking of harmony and perfect health, he never mentioned his trouble by name.

I strongly suggest that you cease talking about your ailments or giving them a name. The only sap from which they draw life is your attention and fear of them. Like the above mentioned psychologist, become a mental surgeon. Then your troubles will be cut off like dead branches are pruned from a tree.

If you are constantly naming your aches and symptoms, you inhibit the kinetic action, which means the release of the healing power and energy of your subconscious mind. Furthermore, by the law of your own mind, these imaginings tend to take shape, *as the thing I greatly feared.* Fill your mind with the great truths of life and walk forward in the light of love.

Lee Pulos adds:

The current thinking among most mind/body doctors is that with every illness, there is an emotion that has not been dealt with or it has been "stuffed." What might the emotion be, (usually anger, stress, etc.,) that has not been dealt with?

Symptoms are a signal from the body/mind that you need to change something in your life. First the body whispers, then it talks, and if not listened to it shouts, and if still not listened to it screams, "too late!"

Summary of your aids to health

1. Find out what it is that heals you. Realize that correct directions given to your subconscious mind will heal your mind and body.
2. Develop a definite plan for turning over your requests or desires to your subconscious mind.
3. Imagine the end desired and feel its reality. Follow it through, and you will get definite results.
4. Decide what belief is. Know that belief is a thought in your mind, and what you think, you create.
5. It is foolish to believe in sickness and something to hurt or to harm you. Believe in perfect health, prosperity, peace, wealth, and divine guidance.
6. Great and noble thoughts upon which you habitually dwell become great acts.
7. Apply the power of prayer therapy in your life. Choose a certain plan, idea, or mental picture. Mentally and emotionally unite with that idea, and as you remain faithful to your mental attitude, your prayer will be answered.
8. Always remember, if you really want the power to heal, you can have it through faith, which means a knowledge of the working of your conscious and subconscious mind. Faith comes with understanding.
9. Blind faith means that a person may get results in healing without any scientific understanding of the powers and forces involved.
10. Learn to pray for your loved ones who may be ill. Quiet your mind, and your thoughts of health, vitality, and perfection operating through the one universal subjective mind will be felt and resurrected in the mind of your loved one.

By 1974 my wife and I began to practice meditation (Transcendental Meditation). Today we still enjoy the many benefits of regular meditation. In my deep meditative state, I integrate my affirmations, as I have learned the subconscious is most responsive to data input when the conscious mind is in its deepest state of relaxation or what is also known as "hypnagogic" state.

As the chapter you have just read describes the power of the subconscious in the facilitation of physical (and mental) healings, let me share one personal story for which I have no scientific explanations.

In 1981, we were living in Sun Valley, Idaho. I had been feeling under the weather, had a sore throat, and didn't seem to be getting any better (very unusual for me). I saw a doctor friend of mine who examined me and told me I had an acute case of mononucleosis. In fact, he insisted I be admitted to the hospital overnight for intravenous feedings and whatever else I was given. I was told it could take as long as a month or more to fully recover from whatever I had. This was unacceptable to me as I was to begin a new career the following week, which would result in our moving to Seattle. My physician friend smiled empathetically and said, "Jim, I appreciate your positive attitude, but your red cells and white cells . . ." and then he proceeded to tell me, medically, why it would take so many weeks or months to restore my system to its normal health.

I was very determined to heal my body that night.

I put myself into a deep meditative state and visualized a white light energy healing and restoring my blood cells to normal. I don't think I ever fell asleep, but I was in the deepest state of rest (theta) and for the longest time that I had (or have since) ever experienced. It was quite something.

In the morning, I felt very energized and called my wife asking her to please bring my jogging shoes, shorts, and a tee shirt to the hospital. I asked the nurses to remove the tubes in my arms and told the on-duty doctor I was going for a run. He didn't want me to leave the hospital and told me I wouldn't be able to run 100 feet. And I didn't. I ran eight miles, what Sun Valley residents call the "loop." I felt great!

When I returned to the hospital, my physician friend was there—who kindly told me I was crazy. I asked him to draw blood from my arm and call me at my home when he had the test results. He called me later and asked me to return to the hospital because they had to do another blood test. I returned to the hospital as requested and had a second blood test which also resulted negative for mononucleosis.

He had never seen anything like this before nor had I. There was no scientific explanation for what had occurred. But, at a deeper level, I knew *I had experienced a healing which I believe to have been facilitated through my deep meditation and profound* belief *I would be healed. I didn't make any fanfare over this, but simply said, "Thank you, God," and went about my work.*

Now, as I read Dr. Murphy's words nearly 30 years later, I more fully understand the dynamics which created that healing and truly experienced the power of my subconscious mind.

The point will be made that all healings are the result of the acceptance of one basic fact: That matter is formed by those inner
qualities that give it vitality, that structure follows expectation,
that matter at any time can be completely changed by the activa-
tion of the creative faculties inherent in all consciousness.

The Nature of Personal Reality, by Jane Roberts

*Roberts, op. cit., p. 13

12

The Tendency of the Subconscious Is Lifeward

In Chapter 7, I briefly introduced the supraconscious. *I wrote:*

The supraconscious is our source of pure creativity. It is that area that we receive great inspiration and creative solutions in which information needed to solve the situation transcends any data stored in our subconscious, or memory bank. "Geniuses" seem to have an ability to tap into this vast reservoir at will.

I also wrote, "Dr. Murphy does not make reference to the supraconscious. Most of the work in this area of study has been done since Dr. Muphy wrote his work in 1963."

Going forward in this book I will substitute "supraconscious" (in italics) where Dr. Murphy has written "subconscious" if it is as the supraconscious has been defined in this book (Chapter 13 describes the functions and characteristics of the supraconscious in detail).

Over 90 percent of your mental life is subconscious, so men and women who fail to make use of this marvelous power live within very narrow limits.

Your subconscious processes are always lifeward and constructive. Your subconscious is the builder of your body and maintains all its vital functions. It is on the job 24 hours a day and never sleeps. It is always trying to help and preserve you from harm.

Your *supraconscious* mind is in touch with infinite life and boundless wisdom, and its impulses and ideas are always lifeward. The great aspirations, inspirations, and visions for a grander and nobler life spring from the *supraconscious*. Our profoundest convictions are those you cannot argue about rationally because they do not come from your conscious mind; they come from your *supraconscious* mind. Your *supraconscious* speaks to you in intuitions, impulses, hunches, intimations, urges, and ideas, and it is always telling you to rise, transcend, grow, advance, adventure, and move forward to greater heights. The urge to love, to save the lives of others comes from the depths of your *supraconscious*. For example, during the great San Francisco earthquake and fire of April 18, 1906, invalids and cripples who had been confined to bed for long periods of time, rose up and performed some of the most amazing feats of bravery and endurance. The intense desire welled up within them to save others at all costs, and their *supraconscious* responded accordingly.

Great artists, musicians, poets, speakers, and writers tune in with their *supraconscious* powers and become animated and inspired. For example, Robert Louis Stevenson, before he went to sleep, used to charge his *supraconscious* with the task of evolving stories for him while he slept. He was accustomed to ask his *supraconscious* to give him a good, marketable thriller when his bank account was low. Stevenson said the intelligence of his deeper mind gave him the story piece by piece, like a serial. This shows how your *supraconscious* will speak lofty and wise sayings through you which your conscious mind knows nothing about.

Mark Twain confided to the world on many occasions that he never worked in his life. All his humor and all his great writings were due to the fact that he tapped the inexhaustible reservoir of his supraconscious mind.

In Dr. Murphy's example of how Robert Louis Stevenson accessed his supraconscious, what is interesting is that solutions that "come to us" from this area of the mind are complete. They are total solutions. When Stevenson wrote another chapter or verse for one of his books, he did not have to edit or rewrite what he had put on paper. He was quoted as saying, "The Brownies come in my sleep and write it."

Other famous creators credit the supraconscious for their creations. Mozart started writing music at the age of three. He published his first sonata at the age of six. He was not a "composer" by his own proclamation. "Music came to me. I am a transcriber of music, not a composer."

He would hear the string section of the music and write it down. He would then hear the brass, piano, and other instruments and "transcribe" what he heard. When completed, the score he had transcribed was perfect. No need for revision. You may recall in the movie Amadeus, there was a great attempt to make Mozart a fraud because those who composed music said it

*was "impossible" to just create a musical score in one sitting with no altera-
tions or rewriting.*

*Beethoven said, "Those moments when full and rich, music comes to my
inner ear." Later in life when he was totally deaf, he produced some of his
best music.*

*Stravinsky stated, "I heard and I wrote what I heard. I was a channel for
the music."*

*Ralph Waldo Emerson used automatic writing. "I sit at my desk, take pen
in hand and an alien force seizes my arm and guides it in writing my material
which I generally read with great interest not knowing that I had known these
things."*

Imagination is far more important than knowledge.

Albert Einstein

How the body portrays the workings of the mind

The interaction of your conscious and subconscious mind requires a similar interaction between the corresponding system of nerves. The cerebrospinal system is the organ of the conscious mind, and the sympathetic
system is the organ of the subconscious mind. The cerebrospinal system is
the channel through which you receive conscious perception by means of
your five physical senses and exercise control over the movement of your
body. This system has its nerves in the brain, and it is the channel of your
volitional and conscious mental action.

The sympathetic system, sometimes referred to as the involuntary
nervous system, has its center in a ganglionic mass at the back of the
stomach known as the solar plexus, and is sometimes spoken of as the abdominal brain. It is the channel of that mental action which unconsciously
supports the vital functions of the body. This is why we often say, "What
does your gut tell you?"

The two systems may work separately or synchronously. Judge Thomas
Troward* says, "The vagus nerve passes out of the cerebral region as a portion of the voluntary system, and through it we control the vocal organs; then

*The Edinburgh Lectures on Mental Science. *New York: Robert McBride & Co., 1909.*

it passes onward to the thorax sending out branches to the heart and lungs; finally, passing through the diaphragm, it loses the outer coating which distinguishes the nerves of the voluntary system and becomes identified with those of the sympathetic system, so forming a connecting link between the two and making the man physically a single entity.

"Similarly different areas of the brain indicate their connection with the objective and subjective activities of the mind respectively, and speaking in a general way we may assign the frontal portion of the brain to the former and the posterior portion to the latter, while the intermediate portion partakes of the character of both."

There is an intelligence which takes care of the body

When you study the cellular system and the structure of the organs, such as eyes, ears, heart, liver, bladder, etc., you learn they consist of groups of cells which form a group intelligence whereby they function together and are able to take orders and carry them out in deductive function at the suggestion of the master mind (conscious mind).

A careful study of the single-celled organism shows you what goes on in your complex body. Though the mono-cellular organism has no organs, it still gives evidence of mind action and reaction performing the basic functions of movement, alimentation, assimilation, and elimination.

Many say there is an intelligence which will take care of your body if you let it alone. That is true, but the difficulty is that the conscious mind always interferes with its five-sense evidence based on outer appearances, leading to the sway of false beliefs, fears, and mere opinion. When fear, false beliefs, and negative patterns are made to register in your subconscious mind through psychological, emotional conditioning, there is no other course open to the subconscious mind except to act on the blueprint specifications offered it.

Your subconscious has a life of its own which is always moving toward harmony, health, and peace.

How man interferes with the innate principle of harmony

To think correctly, scientifically, we must know the "Truth." To know the truth is to be in harmony with the infinite intelligence and power of your subconscious mind, which is always moving lifeward.

Every thought or action which is not harmonious, whether through ignorance or design, will result in discord and limitation of all kinds. Scientists inform us that you build a new body every eleven months; so you are really only eleven months old from a physical standpoint. If you build defects back into your body by thoughts of fear, anger, jealousy, and ill will, you have no one to blame but yourself.

You are the sum total of your own thoughts. You can keep from entertaining negative thought and imagery. The ways to get rid of darkness is with light; the way to overcome cold is with heat; the way to overcome negative thoughts is to substitute good thoughts. Affirm the good, and the bad will vanish.

Why it's normal to be healthy, vital, and strong— it's abnormal to be sick

The average child born into the world is perfectly healthy with all its organs functioning perfectly. This is the normal state, and we should remain healthy, vital, and strong. The instinct of self-preservation is the strongest instinct of your nature, and it constitutes a most potent, ever-present, and constantly operative truth, inherent in your nature. It is, therefore, obvious that all your thoughts, ideas, and beliefs must operate with greater potentiality when they are in harmony with the innate life-principle in you, which is forever seeking to preserve and protect you along all lines. It follows from this that normal conditions can be restored with greater ease and certainty than abnormal conditions can be induced.

It is abnormal to be sick; it simply means you are going against the stream of life and thinking negatively. The law of life is the law of growth; all nature testifies to the operation of this law by silently, constantly expressing itself in the law of growth. Where there is growth and expression, there must be life; where there is life there must be harmony, and where there is harmony, there is perfect health.

If your thought is in harmony with the creative principle of your subconscious mind, you are in tune with the innate principle of harmony. If you entertain thoughts which are not in accordance with the principle of harmony, these thoughts cling to you, harass you, worry you, and finally bring about disease, and if persisted in, possible death.

In the healing of disease, you must increase the inflow and distribution of the vital forces of your subconscious mind throughout your system. This can be done by eliminating thoughts of fear, worry, anxiety, jealousy, hatred, and every other destructive thought which tends to tear down and destroy your nerves and glands—body tissue which controls the elimination of all waste material.

Pointers to review

1. Your subconscious is the builder of your body and is on the job 24 hours a day. You interfere with its life-giving patterns by negative thinking.
2. Charge your *supraconscious* with the task of evolving an answer to any problem, prior to sleep and it will answer you.
3. Watch your thoughts. Every thought accepted as true is sent by your brain to your solar plexus—your abdominal brain—and is brought into your world as a reality.
4. Know that you can remake yourself by giving a new blueprint to your subconscious mind.
5. The tendency of your subconscious is always lifeward. Your job is with your conscious mind. Feed your subconscious mind with premises which are true. Your subconscious is always reproducing according to your habitual mental patterns.
6. You build a new body every eleven months. Change your body by changing your thoughts and keeping them changed.
7. It is normal to be healthy. It is abnormal to be ill. There is within the innate principle of harmony.

8. Thoughts of jealousy, fear, worry, and anxiety tear down and destroy your nerves and glands bringing about mental and physical diseases of all kinds.

9. What you affirm consciously and feel as true will be made manifest in your mind, body and affairs. Affirm the good and enter into the joy of living.

Key 6

CREATIVE PROBLEM SOLVING

Understanding the miraculous
power of your Supraconscious,
the third area of the mind.

13

The Supraconscious and
Creative Problem Solving

The most essential part of the Self is the supraconscious, not ordinarily accessible to conscious awareness. Access to the supraconscious may be enhanced by meditative disciplines, life crises, attitudes (e.g., nonattachment), autosuggestive approaches, ritual, etc.

—Willis Harman*

The supraconscious is such an important part of our overall being that it must be included in any discussion of truly creative problem solving.

It is important to understand that the conscious area of the mind, the subconscious, and the supraconscious are all spheres of our one mind. They each have their own specific functions. The functions of the conscious and the subconscious were explained in detail in Chapter 7. As promised, we will now delve more deeply into the supraconscious and provide you with a step-by-step procedure for engaging the supraconscious in creative problem solving.

First, let's examine the functions and characteristics of the supraconscious.

1. **The supraconscious is the source of all pure creativity.**
   • The conscious area of the mind cannot create. It extrapolates data already stored in the subconscious or accesses data and information from other sources, such as people ("experts"), books, computers, etc.
   • The conscious mind, through deductive reasoning, can solve problems when it accesses data that provides solutions to such problems.

*Harman, Willis and Rheingold, Howard. Higher Creativity: Liberating the Unconscious for Breakthrough Insights: Tarcher, 1984.

- *The supraconscious has access to data not stored in the subconscious. It literally has access to universal knowledge which leads to "pure creativity" beyond the normal reasoning of the conscious and subconscious. We gave examples in the previous chapter of those artists whose creations (music, writings, et al.) came **to** them, not **from** them.*

  Conclusion: The idea(s) comes through on the level the conscious mind is working on (and desires).
  —music to musicians
  —gadgets to inventors
  —prose to writers, etc.

2. **The supraconscious is capable of goal-oriented motivation.**
   There are two types of motivation:
   A. *Constructive motivation—this is when we are driven to achieve or attain something we really* want *to happen.*
   B. *Restrictive motivation—this is doing something we have to do, which may often be the desire or need of someone else, such as our employer, parent, teacher, et al. It is not our desire (to do), but we do it because we have to.*

   The supraconscious provides free-flowing energy only when we are constructively motivated. We seldom get tired doing those things we love to do, while getting exhausted doing those things we "have to do."
   It is important that we align our goals with constructive motivation and wherever possible reduce or eliminate our "have to-s." Even changing our self talk from "I have to" to "I choose to" reduces or eliminates the energy drain from being restrictively motivated.

3. **The supraconscious operates on a non-conscious level.**
   —You can't watch it.
   —There is no place to look for it.

4. **The supraconscious has its own separate computer which will solve any problem assigned to it by the conscious mind, returning the best possible solution at that time.**

   "At that time" is important. If you choose not to use the solution when you receive it, you may want to re-ask your supraconscious for the solution to your problem as additional variables may be added to the equation with the passing of time. The supraconscious may return to you the same solution

you previously received, or a new solution more relevant to your problem or situation as it now stands.

You don't need to use the supraconscious to work on every problem; 90% of your problems can be solved by the conscious mind once it has accessed the data or information for such a solution.

5. **The supraconscious has instant access to all data stored in the subconscious and can discriminate between valid and invalid data in computing.**

Remember, the data stored in our subconscious is the memory of prior experiences as well as the emotions associated with those experiences. It also contains "facts" that we learned earlier in our lives which may be completely erroneous or irrelevant to our present needs. Yet such erroneous data can often be a blockage to our perceiving the TRUTH, or reality, of a given situation.

The supraconscious can lead us to the truth.

6. **The supraconscious cannot compute on any problem while the conscious mind is occupied with that problem.**

When we "worry a problem to death" and can't seem to let go of it (at the conscious level), we block the supraconscious from providing the answer we desire and need. We will show you how to constructively turn the problem over to the supraconscious in this chapter.

Worrying is a great waste of time! (literally). When we have tried repeatedly to solve the problem at the conscious level but seem unable to do so, we turn the problem over to the supraconscious knowing that we will receive the perfect answer/solution. We then become detached from the problem at the conscious level.

Great solutions come to us from the supraconscious during moments of leisure and (mental) relaxation.

Repeating:
The supraconscious cannot compute on any problem while the conscious mind is occupied with that problem.

7. **The supraconscious contains all monitor circuits.**

Here's an experience you have all had many times. Let's say you normally wake up every morning around 6:00 a.m. But tomorrow morning you are going on vacation, and you have an early morning flight and need to be awakened by 4:00 a.m. You set the alarm and may even call a friend who might be traveling with you and ask her if she wouldn't mind calling you at 4:00 a.m., as well. And as you crawl into bed you are telling yourself how important it is to get up at four. The internal dialogue is a request from the conscious to the supraconscious to be awakened at 4:00 a.m. You drift into a deep sleep and a few hours later you wake up with a start. You know it is much earlier than you normally wake up because it is still dark, you roll over on your side to look at your digital clock which reads 3:59 a.m. You reach over to turn off the alarm just as the clock moves to 4:00 and simultaneously the clock starts to buzz just as your hand turns off the alarm. You turn on the light, sit on the edge of the bed thinking about your fun vacation you are about to begin, and the phone rings with your friend telling you it's time to get up. But who really woke you up? Your supraconscious woke you up because those were the instructions you gave it before you went to sleep.

The supraconscious never sleeps. The supraconscious contains all monitor circuits.

8. **The supraconscious makes all of our actions and their effects fit into a pattern consistent with the level of our self concept.**

If our self concept pertaining to memory is, "I can never remember names," the supraconscious will deliberately block our receiving the person's name in order "to make our effects fit into a pattern consistent with the level of our self concept."

Remember, our self concept determines our level of performance in any area of our life (see Chapter 4).

If we don't change the "picture of our self" recorded in our subconscious, we will continue to act in the same way, over and over. The key is to change the picture. And we do that with our own self talk using the affirmation process and techniques (see Chapter 8).

As stated previously, the basic operating principle is:

Any thought, whether positive or negative, held on a continuing basis in the conscious mind, must be brought into reality by the supraconscious mind.

William James (paraphrased)

WE ARE FULLY RESPONSIBLE FOR EVERYTHING THAT HAPPENS IN OUR LIVES.

Yes, there are accidents, but very few. Our lives work much better when we take responsibility and accountability for all of our actions.

Five Steps To Creative Problem Solving

The following is how we precisely engage the supraconscious to help us solve those problems where we seem to be at a "dead end" in finding a relevant answer or solution.

1. *Define the problem.*
2. *Gather data.*
3. *Attempt to solve the problem consciously.*
4. *If unable to solve the problem at the conscious level, turn the problem over to the supraconscious.*
5. *Get your conscious mind busy elsewhere.*

In his wonderful book, The Effective Executive,* *Peter Drucker differentiates between efficiency and effectiveness. He writes, "Efficiency is the ability to do things right. Effectiveness is the ability to do the right things." He states if an executive has to make 100 decisions, there may only be five of those that have any material outcome on the business.*

The point being, you don't need a supercomputer to count your change. Likewise, you don't need to engage the supraconscious to work on every problem.

So again, the five steps of creative problem solving are:

1. **Define the problem.**
   - *Write it down.*
   - *Make sure you clarify the problem and know <u>exactly</u> what it is that needs resolution.*
   - *Dr. Gardner Murphy, a distinguished psychologist and president of the American Society for Psychical Research, stated, "Sixty-five percent of my problems are correctly solved and I get the very best possible solutions as soon as the problem is correctly defined."*

2. **Gather Data.**
   - *This could be data from your own experience stored in your subconscious.*
   - *You may engage a consultant or the "experts."*
   - *Research written data from books, reports, computer information, etc.*

*Drucker, Peter F, The Effective Executive: Guide to Getting the Right Things Done. Harper Paperbooks; Revised Edition, 2006

This whole process should not take much time. Compulsive information gatherers always need to know "more" before making a decision. They may tend to procrastinate, which is driven from a fear of failure.

3. **Attempt to solve the problem consciously.**

We work on the problem at the conscious level. There are "black and white" problems in which there is only one correct solution, and there are problems that may have multiple solutions in which the applicable skill is the ability to prioritize the best possible solution.

In step 3, speed is of the essence. Most problems will be solved in these first three steps, at the conscious level.

4. **If unable to solve the problem at the conscious level, turn the problem over to the supraconscious.**

When do you turn it over to the supraconscious?

When you find yourself repeating possible solutions. In other words, you have clearly defined the problem. You have done a thorough job of gathering information. You have listed all the possible solutions you can think of but nothing you have been able to come up with is the solution.

How do you turn it over to the supraconsicous?
   a) *You mentally repeat the definition of the problem.*
   b) *You ask your supraconscious to take over the problem and return the best possible solution knowing that when you have turned it over, it is solved.*
   c) *If a due date is needed, inform the supraconscious of such.*

5. **Get your conscious mind busy elsewhere.**
   a) *Detach from the problem at the conscious level. Go "play golf." Creativity is a product of leisure.*
   b) *Don't take the problem back (at the conscious level) to see what progress is being made.*

As we say, "Don't dig up the corn." Once you have turned it over to the supraconscious, have the same faith as the farmer who plants his seeds in the spring and trusts that he will have a robust harvest in the fall.

How do you know when you have a supraconscious solution?

No church bells will ring. There will be no visions of angels or colored smoke. But, you will know it came to you from the supraconscious because it will be a total solution. There will be no loose strings. You may have a silly feeling of chagrin, or a "blinding flash of the obvious." What's interesting is your own self talk might say, "Why didn't I think of that!"

The solution will usually come to you when you are doing something passive. You might be driving, day dreaming, or having just awoken from a good night's sleep.

I have personally gone to meetings with others depending on me for an answer to a problem. I have arrived at the meeting without the solution, but still trusting when it is my turn to speak, the answer will appear. As I open my mouth and noise starts to emerge, the perfect solution appears. Even knowing how this material works, I am as amazed as everyone else. It works almost every time.

Where does the information come from, you might ask.

One theory is Carl Jung's collective unconscious, in which he theorizes that at some level of deeper consciousness we all have potential contact with every person in the universe. This is where the theories of E.S.P. and mental telepathy are applicable. Just because we can't see something doesn't mean it doesn't exist.

More advanced science would reveal how we are able to tap into the quantum field of information.

Ralph Waldo Emerson refers to this as the universal pool of all knowledge, which at some deeper level of consciousness we all have access to.

And for some, they may call it God or Divine Intervention.

Regardless of one's beliefs, it all works the same way. The supraconscious and each of our understanding of its incredible power is life changing for many.

Enlightenment involves all questions and problems being turned over to the supraconscious mind which is identical to the one Mind. Answers will then be best not only for the individual, but for all. There are no limits to the supraconscious mind; experienced limits are only the consequences of beliefs about the limits of the human mind.

Integration of the personality implies alignment of conscious with supraconscious choice, so that the whole of one's being— subconscious, conscious, and supraconscious—is conflict free and all directed toward the same ends.

Willis Harman

14

How To Get the Results You Want

The principle reasons for failure are: Lack of confidence and too much effort.

I have made several references in this book to Tim Gallwey. One of the key points I learned from his best selling book, The Inner Game of Tennis, was "that trying interferes with performance." We use to say in our work groups, "Just make it happen." After meeting with Tim, we changed our language to, "Just let it happen!" When we appeared to be stuck on resolving something, we would often say, "Are we efforting too much?"

As Dr. Murphy wrote above, "The principle reasons for failure are: Lack of confidence and too much effort."

Many people block answers to their desires by failing to fully comprehend the workings of their subconscious (and *supraconscious*) mind. When you know how your mind functions, you gain a measure of confidence. You must remember whenever your subconscious mind accepts an idea, it immediately begins to execute it. It uses all its mighty resources to that end and mobilizes all the mental and spiritual laws of your deeper mind (*supraconscious*). This law is true for good or bad ideas. Consequently, if you use it negatively, it brings trouble, failure, and confusion. When you use it constructively, it brings guidance, freedom, and peace of mind.

The right answer is inevitable when your thoughts are positive, constructive, and loving. From this it is perfectly obvious that the only thing you have to do in order to overcome failure is to get your subconscious to accept your idea or request by feeling its reality now, and the law of your mind will do the rest. Turn over your request with faith and confidence, and your subconscious will take over and answer for you.

You will always fail to get results by trying to use mental coercion—your subconscious mind does not respond to coercion, it responds to your faith or conscious mind acceptance.

Your failure to get results may also arise from such statements as: "Things are getting worse." "I will never get an answer." "I see no way out." "It is hopeless." "I don't know what to do." "I'm all mixed up." When you use such statements, you get no response or cooperation from your subconscious mind.

If you get into a taxi and give a half dozen different directions to the driver in five minutes, he would become hopelessly confused and probably would refuse to take you anywhere. It is the same when working with your *supraconscious* mind. There must be a clear-cut idea in your mind. You must arrive at the definite decision that there is a way out, a solution to the vexing problem. Only the infinite intelligence within your *supraconscious* knows the answer. When you come to that clear-cut conclusion in your mind, your mind is then made up, and according to your belief is it done unto you.

Easy does it

A home owner once remonstrated with a furnace repairman for charging two hundred dollars for fixing the boiler by simply supplying a bolt. The mechanic said, "I charge five cents for the missing bolt and one hundred ninety-nine dollars and ninety-five cents for knowing what was wrong."

Similarly, your subconscious mind is the master mechanic, the all-wise one, who knows ways and means of healing any organ of your body, as well as your affairs. Decree health, and your subconscious will establish it, but relaxation is the key. "Easy does it." Do not be concerned with details and means, but know the end result. Get the *feel* of the happy solution to your problem whether it is health, finances, relationships, or employment. Remember how you felt after you had recovered from a severe state of illness. Bear in mind that your feeling is the touchstone of all subconscious demonstration. Your new idea must be felt subjectively in a finished state, not the future, but as coming about now.

Infer no opponent, use imagination and not will power

In using your subconscious mind you infer no opponent, you use no will power. You imagine the end and the freedom state. You will find your intellect trying to get in the way, but persist in maintaining a simple, childlike, miracle-making faith. Picture yourself without the ailment or problem. Imagine the emotional accompaniment of the freedom state you crave. Cut out all red tape from the process. The simple way is the best.

The law of reversed effort and why you get the opposite of what you ask for

Coué, the famous psychologist from France, defined the law of reversed effort as follows: "When your desires and imagination are in conflict, your imagination invariably gains the day."

If, for example, you were asked to walk a plank on the floor, you would do so without question. Now suppose the same plank were placed twenty feet up in the air between two walls, would you walk it? Your desire to walk it would be counteracted by your imagination or fear of falling. Your dominant idea which would be the picture of falling would conquer. Your desire, will, or effort to walk on the plank would be reversed, and the dominant idea of failure would be reinforced.

Mental effort is invariably self-defeated, eventuating always in the opposite of what is desired. The suggestions of powerlessness to overcome the condition dominate the mind; your subconscious is always controlled by the dominant idea. Your subconscious will accept the strongest of two contradictory propositions. The effortless way is the better.

If you say, "I want a healing, but I can't get it," "I try so hard," "I force myself to do my affirmations," "I use all the will power I have," you must realize that your error lies in your effort. Never try to compel the subconscious mind to accept your idea by exercising will power. Such attempts are doomed to failure, and you get the opposite of what you ask for.

The following is a rather common experience. Students, when taking examinations and reading through their papers, find that all their knowledge has suddenly deserted them. Their minds become appalling blanks, and they are unable to recall one relevant thought. The more they grit their teeth and summon the powers of the will, the further the answers seem to flee. But, when they have left the examination room and the mental pressure relaxes, the answers they were seeking flow tantalizingly back into their minds. Trying to force themselves to remember was the cause of their failure. This is an example of the law of reversed effort whereby you get the opposite of what you asked for.

The conflict of desire and imagination must be reconciled

To use mental force is to presuppose that there is opposition. When your mind is concentrated on the means to overcome a problem, it is no longer concerned with the obstacle. When there is no longer any quarrel in either part of your mind, your request will be answered. The two agreeing may also be represented as you and your desire, your thought and feeling, your idea and emotion, your desire and imagination.

You avoid all conflict between your desires and imagination by entering into a drowsy, sleepy state which brings all effort to a minimum. The conscious mind is submerged to a great extent when in a sleepy state. The best time to impregnate your subconscious is prior to sleep. The reason for this is that the highest degree of outcropping of the subconscious occurs prior to sleep and just after we awaken. In this state the negative thoughts and imagery which tend to neutralize your desire and so prevent acceptance by your subconscious mind no longer present themselves. When you imagine the reality of the fulfilled desire and feel the thrill of accomplishment, your subconscious brings about the realization of your desire.

A great many people solve all their dilemmas and problems by the play of their controlled, directed, and disciplined imagination, knowing that whatever they imagine and feel as true *will* and *must* come to pass.

Ideas worth recalling

1. Mental coercion or too much effort shows anxiety and fear which block your answer. Easy does it.
2. When your mind is relaxed and you accept an idea, your subconscious goes to work to execute the idea.
3. Think and plan independently of traditional methods. Know that there is always an answer and a solution to every problem.
4. The feeling of health produces health, the feeling of wealth produces wealth. How do you feel?
5. Imagination is your most powerful faculty. Imagine what is lovely and of good report. You are what you imagine yourself to be.
6. You avoid conflict between your conscious and subconscious in the sleepy state. Imagine the fulfillment of your desire over and over again prior to sleep. Sleep in peace and wake in joy.

15

How to Use the Power of Your Subconscious for Wealth

If you are having financial difficulties, if you are trying to make ends meet, it means you have not convinced your subconscious mind that you will always have plenty and some to spare. You know men and women who work a few hours a week and make fabulous sums of money. They do not strive or slave hard. The effortless way of life is the best. Do the thing you love to do, and do it for the joy and thrill of it.

Wealth is of the mind

Wealth is simply a subconscious conviction on the part of the individual. You will not become a millionaire by saying, "I am a millionaire, I am a millionaire." You will grow into wealth consciousness by building into your mentality the idea of wealth and abundance.

Your invisible means of support

The trouble with most people is that they have no invisible means of support. When business falls away, the stock market drops, or they lose their investments, they seem helpless. The reason for such insecurity is that they do not know how to tap the subconscious mind. They are unacquainted with the inexhaustible storehouse within.

A person with a poverty type mind finds himself in poverty-stricken conditions. Another person with a mind filled with ideas of wealth is surrounded with everything he needs. You can have wealth, everything you need, and plenty to spare. Your words have power to cleanse your mind of wrong ideas and to instill right ideas in their place.

The ideal method for building a wealth consciousness

Perhaps you are saying as you read this chapter, "I need wealth and success." This is what you do: Repeat for about five minutes to yourself three or four times a day, "Wealth—Success." These words have tremendous power. They represent the inner power of the subconscious mind. Anchor your mind on this substantial power within you; then conditions and circumstances corresponding to their nature and quality will be manifested in your life. You are not saying, "I am wealthy," you are dwelling on real powers within you. There is no conflict in the mind when you say, "Wealth." Furthermore, the feeling of wealth will well up within you as you dwell on the idea of wealth.

The *feeling* of wealth produces wealth; keep this in mind at all times. Your subconscious mind is like a bank, a sort of universal financial institution. It magnifies whatever you deposit or impress upon it whether it is the idea of wealth or of poverty. Choose wealth.

Remember the three steps in doing affirmations (Chapter 8):

1. *Read the affirmation to yourself.*
2. *Visually experience a past or future event or an imaginary one that supports your affirmation.*
3. *Inject positive and pleasurable feeling (emotion) into your visualization.*

If one is simply saying, "I am wealthy," without doing steps 2 and 3, their process is incomplete. As we have written, the purpose of language (i.e., step 1) is to create or access an image which supports the words. It has been proven scientifically that it is not the words that record in our subconscious, but the visual images and the feelings associated with those images.

Think of step 3 as the "juice"—the power—that really fires up your image. You could have a beautiful car with a well tuned engine, but with no fuel the car wouldn't go anywhere. The emotional surge you inject into your visual imagery is the "fuel" needed to make this 3-step process effective.

True source of wealth

Your subconscious (*supraconscious*) mind is never short of ideas. There are within it an infinite number of ideas ready to flow into your conscious mind and appear as cash in your pocketbook in countless ways. This process will continue to go on in your mind regardless of whether the stock market goes up or down, or whether the dollar drops in value. Your wealth is never truly dependent on bonds, stocks, or money in the bank; these are really only symbols—necessary and useful, of course, but only symbols.

The point I wish to emphasize is that if you convince your subconscious mind that wealth is yours, and that it is always circulating in your life, you will always and inevitably have it, regardless of the form it takes.

A common stumbling block to wealth

There is one emotion which is the cause of the lack of wealth in the lives of many. Most people learn this the hard way. It is envy. For example, if you see a competitor depositing large sums of money in the bank, and you have only a meager amount of deposit, does it make you envious? The way to overcome this emotion is to say to yourself, "Isn't it wonderful! I rejoice in that man's prosperity. I wish for him greater and greater wealth."

To entertain envious thoughts is devastating because it places you in a very negative position; therefore, wealth flows *from* you instead of *to* you. If you are ever annoyed or irritated by the prosperity or great wealth of another, claim immediately that you truly wish for him greater wealth in every possible way. This will neutralize the negative thoughts in your mind and cause an ever greater measure of wealth to flow to you by the law of your own subconscious mind.

Sleep and grow rich

As you go to sleep at night, practice the following technique. Repeat the word, "Wealth," quietly, easily, and feelingly. Do this over and over again, just like a lullaby. Lull yourself to sleep with the one word, "Wealth." You should be amazed at the result. Wealth should flow to you in avalanches of abundance. This is another example of the magic power of your subconscious mind.

Serve yourself with the powers of your mind

1. Decide to be wealthy the easy way, with the infallible aid of your subconscious mind.

2. Wealth is a subconscious conviction. Build into your mentality the idea of wealth.

3. The trouble with most people is that they have no invisible means of support.

4. Repeat the word, "Wealth," to yourself slowly and quietly for about five minutes prior to sleep and your subconscious will bring wealth to pass in your experience.

5. The feeling of wealth produces wealth. Keep this in mind at all times.

6. Your conscious and subconscious mind must agree. Your subconscious accepts what you really feel to be true. The dominant idea is always accepted by your subconscious mind. The dominant idea should be *wealth,* not *poverty.*

7. You can overcome any mental conflict regarding wealth by affirming frequently, "By day and by night I am being prospered in all of my interests."

8. Stop writing blank checks, such as, "There is not enough to go around," or "There is a shortage," etc. Such statements magnify and multiply your loss.

9. Deposit thoughts of prosperity, wealth, and success in your subconscious mind, and the latter will give you compound interest.

10. What you consciously affirm, you must not mentally deny a few moments later. This will neutralize the good you have affirmed.

11. Your true source of wealth consists of the ideas in your mind. You can have an idea worth millions of dollars. Your subconscious will give you the idea you seek.

12. Envy and jealousy are stumbling blocks to the flow of wealth. Rejoice in the prosperity of others.

Rich versus wealthy

Simply a comment to emphasize the importance of keeping balance in our lives in the pursuit of becoming wealthy. We have all heard the stories of the person who leaves home at 6:00 a.m., before the kids are up and arrives home well after they are in bed. The stress of the "pursuit of wealth" is often accompanied by an unhealthy lifestyle resulting in poor nutrition, little or no exercise, too much drinking and an early trip to Le Cemetery!

It requires money to be wealthy. It requires no money to be "rich." Mother Teresa, Gandhi, and others can be our models of great richness, with no monetary measurements.

Balance is the key in the pursuit of becoming wealthy. Balanced people budget an equal amount of time to pursue their family, health, social, spiritual, and personal goals.

Michael Josephson, founder of The Josephson Institute of Ethics writes:

Acquisition of things is very similar to the taking of drugs: with drugs, the body adjusts very quickly, and you have to keep taking more to get the same effect. The same with sex. The first couple of times is amazing, then it becomes mundane. If you were to list the five happiest people you know, there would be no correlation to income. People who are genuinely happy are not happy because of what they have; they're happy because of their concept of who they are.

16

Your Subconscious Mind
and Happiness

William James said that the greatest discovery of the nineteenth century was not in the realm of physical science. The greatest discovery was the power of the subconscious touched by faith. In every human being is that limitless reservoir of power which can overcome any problem in the world.

True and lasting happiness will come into your life the day you get the clear realization that you can overcome any weakness—the day you realize that your subconscious can solve your problems, heal your body, and prosper you beyond your fondest dream.

You might have felt very happy when your child was born, when you got married, when you graduated from college, or when you won a great victory or a prize. You might have been very happy when you became engaged to the loveliest girl or the most handsome man. You could go on and list innumerable experiences which have made you happy. However, no matter how marvelous these experiences are, they do not give real lasting happiness—they are transitory.

You must choose happiness

Happiness is a state of mind. You have the freedom to choose happiness. This may seem extraordinarily simple, and it is. Perhaps this is why people stumble on their way to happiness; they do not see the simplicity of the key to happiness. The great things of life are simple, dynamic, and creative. They produce well-being and happiness.

He made it a habit to be happy

A number of years ago, I stayed for about a week in a farmer's house in Connemarra on the west coast of Ireland. He seemed to be always singing and whistling and was full of humor. I asked him the secret of his happiness, and his reply was: "It is a habit of mine to be happy. Every morning when I awaken and every night before I go to sleep, I bless my family, the crops, the cattle, and I thank God for a wonderful harvest."

This farmer had made a practice of this for over forty years. As you know, thoughts repeated regularly and systematically sink into the subconscious mind and become habitual. He discovered that happiness is a habit.

You must desire to be happy

There is one very important point about being happy. You must sincerely *desire* to be happy. There are people who have been depressed, dejected, and unhappy so long that were they suddenly made happy by some wonderful, good, joyous news, they would actually be like the woman who said to me, "It is wrong to be so happy!" They have been so accustomed to the old mental patterns that they do not feel at home being happy! They long for the former, depressed, unhappy state.

I knew a woman in England who had rheumatism for many years. She would pat herself on the knee and say, "My rheumatism is bad today. I cannot go out. My rheumatism keeps me miserable."

This dear elderly lady got a lot of attention from her son, daughter, and the neighbors. She really wanted her rheumatism. She enjoyed her "misery" as she called it. This woman did not really want to be happy.

I suggested a curative procedure to her. I wrote down some affirmations and told her that if she gave attention to these truths, her mental attitude would undoubtedly change and would result in her faith and confidence in being restored to health. She was not interested. There seems to be a peculiar, mental, morbid streak in some people, whereby they seem to enjoy being miserable and sad.

Why choose unhappiness?

Many people choose unhappiness by entertaining these ideas: "Today is a black day; everything is going to go wrong." "I am not going to succeed." "Everyone is against me." "Business is bad, and it is going to get worse." "I'm always late." "I never get the breaks." "He can, but I can't." If you have this attitude of mind the first thing in the morning, you will attract all these experiences to you, and you will be very unhappy.

Begin to realize that the world you live in is determined largely by what goes on in your mind. Marcus Aurelius, the great Roman philosopher and sage, said, "A man's life is what his thoughts make of it." Emerson, America's foremost philosopher, said, "A man is what he thinks about all day long." The thoughts you habitually entertain in your mind have the tendency to actualize themselves in physical conditions.

Make certain you do not indulge in negative thoughts, defeatist thoughts, or unkind, depressing thoughts. Recall frequently to your mind that you can experience nothing outside your own mentality.

He found happiness to be the harvest of a quiet mind

Lecturing in San Francisco some years ago, I interviewed a man who was very unhappy and dejected over the way his business was going. He was the general manager. His heart was filled with resentment toward the vice president and the president of the organization. He claimed that they opposed him. Because of this internal strife, business was declining; he was receiving no dividends or stock bonuses.

This is how he solved his business problem: The first thing in the morning he affirmed quietly as follows, "All those working in our corporation are honest, sincere, co-operative, faithful, and full of good will to all. They are mental and spiritual links in the chain of this corporation's growth, welfare, and prosperity. I radiate love, peace, and good will in my thoughts, words and deeds to my two associates and to all those in the company. The president and the vice president of our company are divinely guided in all their undertakings. The infinite intelligence of my subconscious mind makes all decisions through me. There is only right action in all our business transactions and in our relationship with each other. I send the messengers of peace, love, and good will before me to the office. Peace and harmony reign supreme in the minds and hearts of all those in the company including myself. I now go forth into a new day, full of faith, confidence, and trust."

This business executive repeated the above meditation slowly three times in the morning, feeling the truth of what he affirmed. When fearful or angry thoughts came into his mind during the day, he would say to himself, "Peace, harmony, and poise govern my mind at all times."

As he continued disciplining his mind in this manner, all the harmful thoughts ceased to come, and peace came into his mind. He reaped the harvest.

Subsequently, he wrote me to the effect that at the end of about two weeks of reordering his mind, the president and the vice president called him into the office, praised his operations and his new constructive ideas, and remarked how fortunate they were in having him as general manager. He was very happy in discovering that man finds happiness within himself.

The block or stump is not really there

I read a newspaper article some years ago which told about a horse who had shied when he came to a stump on the road. Subsequently, every time the horse came to that same stump, he shied. The farmer dug the stump out, burned it, and leveled the old road. Yet, for twenty-five years, every time the horse passed the place where the former stump was, he shied. The horse was shying at the memory of a stump.

There is no block to your happiness save in your own thoughts and mental imagery. Are fear or worry holding you back? Fear is a thought in your mind. You can dig it up this very moment by supplanting it with faith in success, achievement, and victory over all problems.

Summary of steps to happiness

1. William James said that the greatest discovery of the 19th century was the power of the subconscious mind touched by faith.

2. There is tremendous power within you. Happiness will come to you when you acquire a sublime confidence in this power. Then, you will make your dreams come true.

3. When you open your eyes in the morning, say to yourself, I choose happiness today. I choose success today. I choose right action today. I choose love and good will for all today. I choose peace today. Pour life, love, and interest into this affirmation, and you have chosen happiness.

4. You must sincerely desire to be happy. Nothing is accomplished without desire. Desire is a wish with wings of imagination and faith. Imagine the fulfillment of your desire, and feel its reality, and it will come to pass.

5. By constantly dwelling on thoughts of fear, worry, anger, hate, and failure, you will become very depressed and unhappy. Remember, your life is what your thoughts make of it.

6. You cannot buy happiness with all the money in the world. Some millionaires are very happy, some are very unhappy. Many people with very little worldly goods are very happy, and some are very unhappy. The kingdom of happiness is in your thought and feeling.

7. There is no block to your happiness. External things are not causative, these are effects, not cause. Take your cue from the only creative principle within you. Your thought is cause, and a new cause produces a new effect. Choose happiness.

17

Your Subconscious Mind and Harmonious Human Relations

In studying this book, you learn that your subconscious mind is a recording machine which faithfully reproduces whatever you impress upon it. This is one of the reasons for the application of the Golden Rule in human relations. As you would that people should think about you, think you about them in like manner. As you would that people should feel about you, feel you also about them in like manner. As you would want people to act toward you, act you toward them in like manner.

For example, you may be polite and courteous to someone in your office, but when his back is turned, you are very critical and resentful toward him in your mind. Such negative thoughts are highly destructive to you. It is like taking poison. You are actually taking mental poisons which rob you of vitality, enthusiasm, strength, guidance, and good will. These negative thoughts and emotions sink down into your subconscious, and cause all kinds of difficulties and maladies in your life.

The master key to happy relationships with others

To judge others is to think, to arrive at a mental verdict or conclusion in your mind. The thought you have about the other person is your thought, because you are thinking it. Your thoughts are creative, therefore, you actually create in your own experience what you think and feel about the other person. It is also true that the suggestion you give to another, you give to yourself because your mind is the creative medium.

Your subconscious mind is impersonal and unchanging, neither considering persons nor respecting religious affiliations or institutions of any kind. It is neither compassionate nor vindictive. The way you think, feel, and act toward others returns at last upon yourself.

Becoming emotionally mature

What the other person says or does cannot really annoy or irritate you except if you permit her to disturb you. The only way she can annoy you is through your own thought. For example, if you get angry, you have to go through four stages in your mind: You begin to think about what she said. You decide to get angry and generate an emotion of rage. Then, you decide to act. Perhaps, you talk back and react in kind. You see that the thought, emotion, reaction, and action all take place in your mind.

When you become emotionally mature, you do not respond negatively to the criticism and resentment of others. To do so would mean that you had descended to that state of low mental vibration and become one with the negative atmosphere of the other. Identify yourself with your aim in life, and do not permit any person, place, or thing to deflect you from your inner sense of peace, tranquility, and radiant health.

The meaning of love in harmonious human relations

Sigmund Freud, the Austrian founder of psychoanalysis, said that unless the personality has love, it sickens and dies. Love includes understanding, good will, and respect for the other person. The more love and good will you emanate and exude, the more comes back to you.

If you puncture the other fellow's ego and wound his estimate of himself, you cannot gain his good will. Recognize that every person wants to be loved and appreciated, and made to feel important in the world. Realize that the other person is conscious of their worth, and that, like yourself, feels the dignity of being an expression of the One Life Principle animating all people. As you do this consciously and knowingly, you build the other person up, and your love and good will are returned to you.

Appeasement never wins

Give no one in the world the power to deflect you from your goal, your aim in life, which is to express your hidden talents to the world, to serve humanity, and to reveal more and more of your God-given wisdom, truth, and beauty to all people in the world. Remain true to your ideal. Know definitely and absolutely that whatever contributes to your peace, happiness, and fulfillment must of necessity bless all who walk the earth. The harmony of the part is the harmony of the whole, for the whole is in the part, and the part is in the whole. All you owe the other is love, and love is the fulfilling of the law of health, happiness, and peace of mind.

Profitable pointers in human relations

1. Your subconscious mind is a recording machine which reproduces your habitual thinking. Think good of the other, and you are actually thinking good about yourself.
2. A hateful or resentful thought is a mental poison. Do not think ill of another, for to do so is to think ill of yourself. You are the only thinker in your universe, and your thoughts are creative.
3. Your mind is a creative medium; therefore, what you think and feel about the other, you are bringing to pass in your own experience. This is the psychological meaning of the Golden Rule. As you would that man should think about you, think you about them in the same manner.
4. The good you do, the kindness proffered, the love and good will you send forth, will all come back to you multiplied in many ways.
5. You are the only thinker in your world. You are responsible for the way you think about the other. Remember, the other person is not responsible for the way you think about him. Your thoughts are reproduced. What are you thinking now about the other person?
6. Become emotionally mature and permit other people to differ from you. They have a perfect right to disagree with you, and you have the same freedom to disagree with them. You can disagree without being disagreeable.

7. Animals pick up your fear vibrations and snap at you. If you love animals, they will never attack you. Many undisciplined human beings are just as sensitive as dogs, cats, and other animals.

8. Your inner speech, representing your silent thoughts and feelings, is experienced in the reactions of others toward you.

9. Wish for the other what you wish for yourself. This is the key to harmonious human relations.

10. The other person cannot annoy you or irritate you unless you permit him. Your thought is creative; you can bless him.

11. Love is the answer to getting along with others. Love is understanding, good will, and respecting the other.

12. Rejoice in the success, promotion, and good fortune of the other. In doing so, you attract good fortune to yourself.

13. All you owe any person in the world is love, and love is wishing for everyone what you wish for yourself—health, happiness, and all the blessings of life.

Non-Judgment Day Is Near

How many of us like to be judged? I don't, and I assume you do not, either.

People don't like to be judged—especially prejudged. We seek first to be understood. With understanding we hope to become appreciated, valued, and ultimately loved. But, not judged.

Recently, I read a short page in a HeartMath newsletter written by staff member, Kim Allen. Kim wrote:

A college friend of mine used to believe the small peephole in our sorority house front door was put there for blind dates. She'd look through the small hole and immediately decide whether or not the rest of the evening would be worth her time.

On a few occasions, rather than open the door for a full view, she'd let the prejudged and unsuspecting young man walk away believing no one was home.

Most of us would rather not be on the receiving end of a judgment because we don't like the way it feels. Yet how often do we see others through self-imposed peepholes? We rarely consider that the act of judging or blaming someone else can

have the same ill effects on the transmitter as it has on the re-
ceiver: stress.

The other night my wife and I went to one of our favorite Seattle res-
taurants. This restaurant is located across the street from the hotel we have
stayed at for the past 13 years prior to moving back to Seattle in 2006. Over
the years we have come to know the staff of this restaurant. Their consistent,
warm greetings and remembering of our names always make us feel wel-
come and appreciated.

One of the managers, however, (whom I will call "Tommy") always
seemed to be ambivalent about our arrival and never greeted us or acknowl-
edged our presence. I developed the feeling he didn't really care if we pa-
tronized his establishment or not. Over several years I began to feel he either
didn't like us or he was just cold and unfriendly. The latter seemed inconsis-
tent with his friendly and upbeat staff.

This particular evening we arrived early, before the dinner crowd, and
took a seat in one of the booths in the nearly empty bar. After Tommy had
made three or four passes by our booth without saying hello or acknowledg-
ing us, I decided to confront him to see if there was something we might have
said or done at one time that upset him. So, on his next pass I said, "Tommy,
could you sit down and join us for a few minutes?" He sat down next to me
and across from my wife.

I then said, "Tommy, as you know, Jeri and I have been coming here for
over 20 years. We congratulate you on the development and retention of
such a friendly and capable staff. But, I have a question. You never greet
us or say hello, and I have developed the feeling you would just as soon
we not even visit you. I simply want to know if I have said something or
done something that may have upset you. And, if so, I would like to clear
things up."

After a pause, Tommy turned toward me with a big smile and said, "Jim,
there is something you don't know about me. I am legally blind. I don't even
see you (or anyone else) when you come in here and if I don't recognize your
"voice print," I have no way of knowing you are here."

It was my turn to pause. I then started laughing and said, "That is the
greatest story I have heard. Tommy, I have been prejudging you for some
time based on totally erroneous data and input from my own conscious mind.
In fact, you have inspired me to include this story in my book." We all had a
good laugh, which resulted in a love-in.

Now when we visit the restaurant and see Tommy, I go out of my way to go to him and say, "Hey Tommy, it's Jim and Jeri. How are things going?" And, we always have a fun and friendly chat.

Judgment: It made me introspectively ask myself the question, how often have I been quick to arrive at a conclusion with very limited or false information. And, almost every time I have done so my conclusions and opinions end up being wrong.

As Kim Allen concludes:

One of the quickest ways to eliminate judgments and blame is sincere appreciation. Like other positive emotional states, appreciation improves human performance, including the way the brain processes information. It allows the cortical facilitation and the ability to see situations, and others, from a broader perspective.

So the next time you find yourself rushing to a judgment, open the door. Find something to appreciate instead. You'll feel better. More importantly, you'll start to see others, and the situation, in a completely different light.

Thank you, Kim. Non judgment day is near.

18

From Me to We: Principles of Enlightened Leadership

Have you ever wondered how some people seem to like almost everyone while others are often grouchy and constantly critical of every little thing?

In the 2011 football season, I attended the Seattle Seahawks-St. Louis Rams football game, which Seattle won, giving them the Division Championship. I haven't met the Seahawks head coach, Pete Carroll, but I have great admiration for his consistent, upbeat attitude. He just seems to always be positive and expects positive outcomes. Having participated in team sports, I have always thought Coach Carroll would be a fun coach to play for.

In the world of business, much has been written about corporate cultures and the impact they can have (positive or negative) on a company's success. I have been blessed to have been part of the management of companies where the leadership was trained to "catch an employee" doing something right (rather than wrong), and then reinforcing such behavior with praise and positive reinforcement.

These are fun companies to work for where, management is constantly acknowledging the members in their work unit for all their positive, successful results. It doesn't mean that mistakes don't occur or that there is never constructive criticism. And, in some cases an employee may need to be replaced. It simply means the general atmosphere within the work place is very positive. In these environments, work becomes fun.

The reputation of companies who place high value on the quality of their employees, and a work place that fosters personal growth in addition to employee training, also attracts employees with high self esteem. People much prefer being valued and appreciated as opposed to being criticized and denigrated. The same is true outside the work place.

Some managers just seem to get up on the wrong side of the bed every morning and come to work with an attitude of trying to catch people doing things wrong so they can be reprimanded and "put in their place." Managers with such attitudes usually have a low self concept, and their M.O. is to try to make themselves look important by putting others down. Then they wonder why they just can't find "good people" to work for their company. Only people with low self concepts would subject themselves to working in such a negative environment. And for them, it's only about receiving a pay check. "Fun" is what happens away from work. Unfortunately, the same people who manage their companies with such negative attitudes often manage their families and personal friendships with the same arrogance and disrespect.

The best leaders I know have excellent human relations skills. They genuinely like people. It is their attitude, *and attitudes are all a matter of personal choice. So, why wouldn't we choose to value high human relations skills? Life becomes so much more fun and things come together more effortlessly because good teams are the result of shared visions, with each team member embracing both their individual goals as well as the goals of their fellow teammates.*

Two excellent affirmations to help develop a high sense of human relations are:

"I have unconditional warm regards for all people at all times."

and,

"I am truly self determined and allow others the same right!"

In the first affirmation, the word "all" is used for emphasis. Certainly we would not have "warm regards" for a psychopath or someone who caused us great harm.

The most important words in the second affirmation are, "and allow others the same right!" Many people are self determined, but don't allow others the same right. These people tend to be consistently disagreeable. When we "allow others the same right," we can agree to disagree without becoming disagreeable.

Having a personal goal to develop great human relations is a very worthy goal and will add greatly to the value of those lives who embrace such a tenet.

Leaders of companies and organizations, who have great human relations skills, truly value and like their employees. not just as employees but as people.

I haven't met Tony Hsieh, the CEO of Zappos, but I was very inspired reading his book, Delivering Happiness.* *Although birthed as a customer experi-*

---

*Hsieh, Tony, Delivering Happiness. *Hachette Book Group: June, 2010*

ence, Tony and his team extended Delivering Happiness to the employees, their families, vendors, shareholders and everyone Zappos has the opportunity to touch. Tony really gets it! (I highly recommend his book.)

These kinds of "new age" management styles and corporate cultures were not a subject of much discussion within companies 50 years ago. Most management styles were traditional, managed from the top down, and had little interest or patience in hearing ideas or receiving input from the workforce. This attitude fostered the rapid growth of labor unions. The organizational hierarchy was sacrosanct and most employees lived in fear of upsetting the "boss."

In today's successful organizations that have transcended the old style management paradigm, there is an almost inverted pyramid where enlightened leaders understand the value and importance of "working for" those who "report to" them. They are constantly receiving input and feedback from their employees, so they can better understand the problems and issues one might be challenged with to be more productive in his work. The leader sees his/her role as helping to eliminate barriers and obstacles to heightened performance.

Let me share a model that differentiates why people may have sought positions of leadership in the past compared to what is evolving in 21st century leadership.

Old Paradigm	*New Paradigm*
Personal Power	*Empower Others*
To Control	*To Influence*
To Be Served	*To Serve Others*

Many books have been written about organizational development and management structure and style. For a moment, reflect that in the year 1900 over 90% of the workforce in the United States was in agriculture. They were mostly male farmers. The industrial revolution was just beginning to birth. Within 15 years the young men of that same class were enlisting or being drafted into the armed services to serve in World War I. For many, the armed services was their first "model" of management.

By necessity, this was a top-down model. In order for things to work there had to be clear understanding of rank. One was taught to respect the uniform (title) as much as the person who wore it. Again, completely understandable (and appreciated). When under enemy fire, it was not a consideration to build "consensus thinking" or "survey the employees" to get their input and ideas. We won the war largely because of very strong leadership, great strategic planning at the top, and a military who followed orders as directed.

So, what is the relevance here to organizational development?

When our soldiers returned home, there was a great migration of families moving from the farmlands to the big cities. It was easy for these young men to slide into companies and corporations who had similar management structures. Even language learned in the military became common within the workplace, such as:

- *"We're under the gun to get this done."*
- *"We're on the firing line to achieve our quota."*
- *"Make sure you're well armed when you attend that meeting."*
- *"We need to attack our competition with full force. They are the enemy!"*
- *"This is not the time to retreat."*
- *And, "You're fired!"*
- *Etc., etc., etc.*

The primary motivations for people to become leaders in the old management paradigm were to have personal power, to control others, and to be served by the workforce. Communication was strictly top down. Titles were very important and God forbid you should question a person of higher authority.

"Jensen, you don't talk to vice presidents that way!" It was not uncommon for bosses to strut their power by dressing down an underling with a loud voice in the presence of fellow workers. Human Resource departments and notions of harassment didn't exist.

The primary mood within the company was fear-based. Fear that you might do or say the wrong thing that could lead to your getting fired. The environment was suppressive. And, beneath the external veneer of the macho boss was a person also driven by fear and doubt. Fear of failure and fear of others learning of his own insecurities and doubts as to whether he really had the "right stuff" to succeed.

These kinds of environments attracted workers with a predominantly low self concept. They literally felt "worth-less" and since their primary motivation was survival, they just kept their mouths shut and did what they were told to do.

As time progressed, more and more people were able to attend college and the general education level increased. In the 1950s there became an emergence of seminars, books, and teachings that dealt with the subject of self discovery and the importance of developing one's self concept and self esteem.

We began to see the emergence of more and more enlightened leaders. Leaders who truly recognized the ingenuity of the human spirit in all people. Leaders whose self concepts were well intact and who appreciated and valued that creative ideas and solutions could come from anywhere within the organization. They created environments that fostered openness and developed reward and recognition systems for such valued contributions.

More and more leaders began to perceive themselves as teachers and mentors. Instead of seeking personal power, they recognized the value of empowering others. Rather than controlling their employees, they were inspired to influence them. They realized when you control someone you no longer influence him. As a parent, for example, would you rather control your children or influence them? I hope the answer is obvious.

And lastly, the enlightened leader was not into being served by others but rather being of service to his or her fellow workers.

Which work environment would you choose to work in? Another question that I presume the answer is obvious.

When leaders clearly embrace these values and principles, they don't possess their employees. They may take ownership in helping facilitate the success of others (another value), but they know they don't own them. Promotions and advancements, even when it results in the employee leaving the company to go elsewhere or start his/her own company, are greeted with praise and congratulations.

I am reminded of a quote from the book, Flow,* *where the author writes,*

Ideal teachers (i.e., managers) act as bridges over which they invite their students to cross. Once having facilitated the crossing, they joyfully collapse allowing their students to build bridges of their own.

Csikszentmihalyi, Mihaly, Flow: The Psychology of Optimal Experience. *Harper Perennial Modern Classics: July, 2008*

19

Constructive Criticism, Dealing with Mistakes, and the Perils of Perfectionism

If I was addressing a large audience and asked the question, "How many of you like to be criticized?" a very small percentage would probably raise their hands.

Criticism, when properly defined and well intended, can be an excellent teaching tool. But first we need to define the word itself and differentiate between constructive and destructive criticism. Then, how we administer the criticism is essential—our focus must remain on particular behavior or procedure while leaving intact the self esteem of the individual being criticized.

Let's define criticism.

Destructive criticism devalues the individual being criticized.

Constructive (or informational) criticism teaches the individual being criticized. If I were to re-ask my question, "How many of you like to be criticized?" and your understanding of the term criticism was, "an objective assessment of your behavior or actions with the intention of helping you improve," it is more likely a majority of the audience would raise their hands.

Our problem with the word criticism is that most of our early memories of being criticized were destructive criticism, where we were scolded and told how bad we were for doing something "wrong." We were made to feel guilty or bad about ourselves, often leading to feelings of being worthless. When we are repeatedly criticized by authority figures, our self esteem gets beaten up and our overall self concept is lowered.

Imagine as a small child a giant (i.e., mom or dad) saying to you, "What's the matter with you" over spilling your milk or arriving five minutes late for dinner? This is insane. This parental behavior sets up an internal pattern within the child which screams loudly inside his head, "I hate to be criticized," and, worse yet, devaluing self talk such as, "I can never do anything right" "I will never be as good as my big brother (or sister)," etc., etc. How criticism is handled with children is a significant factor in the raising or lowering of the child's self esteem and self concept. Much adult therapy is spent in unwinding early childhood memories of being told one was bad or no good or literally worthless (i.e., of no worth).

So what do we do when our child does something really unacceptable, like throwing a rock through the neighbor's window or "borrowing" mom's car for a little joy ride when mom and dad are out for the evening? Does this mean there is no punishment for this wrong behavior?

Of course there is punishment, which hopefully is limited to the suspension of privileges or confinement to one's room, etc. Psychological beatings, however, such as yelling and screaming, can have long-term debilitating effects to the person being yelled at.

So what do we do?

The answer is to keep fully focused on the behavior, not the individual himself. "Criticize the deed, not the doer."

For example, "Johnny, what you did is totally unacceptable. We love you, Johnny, but we don't love what you did. That kind of behavior is something we don't do or approve of in our family. You are a good person, Johnny, but what you did is wrong. Let's discuss it."

This is an overstated, oversimplified example. But the message is: when we criticize someone (especially someone we love, such as a child or spouse), we need to be certain our intent is to help or improve a condition of the person being criticized and not just an excuse to vent our own anger or frustration. As a rule of thumb, it is best to defer criticism when we are angry. This is when most destructive criticism occurs.

In business, good leaders and managers develop expertise in constructive or informational criticism. They are able to assist an employee and correct performance in a way that actually increases the self esteem of the person being criticized.

Example: "John, in our review yesterday you stated you wanted to make more money, and in our company that means making more sales. You are a good salesman. But, I have noticed you don't always write down your appointments, and I have heard from some of our accounts you don't return their calls promptly. I used to have that problem myself. Let me share with you the system I developed that has enabled me to be much more effective in managing my calendar. And for me, personally, it resulted in increased sales because by more efficiently managing my time, I was able to actually increase my number of sales calls while maintaining good customer relations by always responding to their needs or inquiries promptly. Let me show you how I did that. You have the potential to be one of our best salespeople, John."

Bottom line on criticism, be firm on issues but easy on people. Again, criticize the deed, not the doer.

So how do we constructively deal with mistakes so we don't beat ourselves up in the process.

Mistakes—an interesting word, which we will discuss in more detail in a moment.

I received a telephone call recently from a friend who began his conversation with, "I want to make amends." When I asked him for what, he stated he had told me he had sent a book to a friend of mine when in reality he hadn't. He said he had sent out two books that day and he thought he had sent one to my friend. He said, "I fibbed."

Another interesting word.

I asked if he had told me he sent the book to my friend and knew he hadn't, or had he actually thought he had sent it but later realized my friend was not who he had sent it to. He responded that he genuinely thought he had sent the book at the time he told me he had. Yet, he sounded terrible and admitted he felt awful.

Frankly, I was flabbergasted.

I said, "You didn't fib, you simply made a mistake. Why are you beating yourself up for making a mistake?"

Unfortunately, many of us have been conditioned, beginning at a very early age, to think that it is bad to make a mistake. This, then, gets internalized as, we are bad. If we spilled our milk, we were scolded. If we dirtied our clothes, we were asked what was wrong with us. If we showed up late for dinner, we were sent to our room. If we forgot to do our homework, we weren't allowed to watch TV. If we did poorly on a test . . . and on and on and on.

Insanity! We were made to believe that not only were mistakes bad, but we were bad if we made them.

Of course, once we grew up we forgot all that nonsense. Right? Wrong.

My friend who called me this morning to "make amends" is in his mid-30s. What happened (in his mind) when he made a simple mistake? How about this: "I made a mistake. That's bad. I'm bad. I fibbed to Jim. I'm a liar. Why do I always screw up?" . . . ad nauseam. You laugh, but that's how many people deal with mistakes.

None of us go through life without making mistakes. But, how we deal with mistakes is essential to our well-being. Some people beat themselves up while others have the ability to laugh at their mistakes.

The other evening my wife and I saw the movie "Showtime" with Eddie Murphy and Robert DeNiro. At the end of the movie and following the rolling of the credits, we were shown the out-takes. As you know these are the humorous occurrences during the making of the movie where the actors screwed up their lines and made a mis-take. In fact, the director is shown saying, "Take two," take three," and however many mis-takes are required to get it right. And, what is the response of the actors who made the mistake? They laugh like hell! So does the rest of the cast and the audience.

We need to lighten our load and not be so serious when we screw up. That doesn't mean we don't accept responsibility. But, we simply admit (to ourselves or others) we made a mistake.

They put erasers on pencils and bumpers on automobiles to help us deal with our mistakes. (If we deliberately ram someone in another car, that is not a mistake. That is a direct hit! There is a difference.)

We can learn from mistakes. It is good to try and avoid making the same mistake over and over. But, let's not beat ourselves up (or someone else whom we love) for making a simple mistake. If necessary, we apologize and get on with it.

"I love myself unconditionally."

'I never devalue myself with destructive criticism."

"I have unconditional warm regards for all people at all times."

The Perils of Perfectionism

Each of you has already, or will have, a relationship of some kind with a perfectionist. It may be a parent, sibling, teacher, coach, friend, or manager—all of whom intend to make you a better person.

Most often, perfectionists have inherited the "value" of perfectionism.

I do not intend, here, to make a judgment about perfectionism, but rather point out my observations, over time, of the burden perfectionists tend to put on those over whom they have the greatest control or influence. If you have or have had perfectionist tendencies, the choice is clearly yours in determining whether or not their continuance will bring you greater joy and happiness and enhance the quality of your own life as well as those who are most important to you.

I believe it is a tremendous burden to be parented or managed by a perfectionist. Seldom will your behavior or performance measure up to the expectation of the perfectionist. And, over time, one's self esteem runs the risk of being knocked down from the constant feeling of not being "good enough" in the eyes of the person who you may love and admire the most. In families especially, the traits of perfectionism tend to get passed from generation to generation.

Is this the time to consider breaking that chain?

The problem with perfectionism is that excellence is seldom good enough. The world view of the perfectionist is focused on what is wrong with things rather than what is right.

Consider the example of a young aspiring gymnast who has the performance of her life. She gets a standing ovation, the judges rate her performance a 9.8, and she wins first place. It would be most natural for her coach to say, "Fantastic performance! You were great! Look at how far you have developed." Words that would, rightfully, make the young gymnast feel really good about her performance and herself.

Now let's look at this same situation and the words that would likely come from the mouth of the perfectionist coach. "Good job. But, let me point out what you need to keep working on, that was the difference between your 9.8 and a 10." He then continues to coach her by pointing out the things she did wrong in her performance. And, although he is intellectually correct in his analysis, he doesn't add to the celebration. The young gymnast leaves the arena thinking of her errors rather than her successes. Over time, this well-intended coach becomes a "psychic bleeder." The psychological effect is that the person being coached feels less worthy about herself, again, for not measuring up to the expectation of the person coaching, teaching, or managing them.

You might ask, "Well, how does the person improve her performance if someone isn't telling her what to work on"?

Good question.

What we are talking about, here, is the process of how one is coached. All coaching is based on enhancing performance.

The non-perfectionist coach, who accepts excellence as his performance standard, might have said something different after the performance of our young gymnast, who we will name Mary.

"Mary, that's the best you have ever done. You were fantastic! I can't wait until Monday when we can watch the tape of your performance together. Great job! Let's celebrate."

The coach may have some constructive thoughts or coaching tips as well. But, he is also genuinely thrilled over Mary's performance, and now is certainly not the time to make additional suggestions. In this approach, Mary leaves her performance thinking to herself, "Wow, I really hit it today. All that training and hard work is paying off. I feel great!" She is left with the opportunity to review all the things she did right. As she lies awake in bed too excited to sleep, she sees in her mind that great dismount, the crowd leaping to their feet, the judges holding up their scores, her teammates and coach hugging her, giving her all those high-fives, etc., etc., etc. She literally feels elated about herself and her self worth.

Monday will come soon enough. And, after viewing the film together with her coach, a good coach might say, "Anything you see there that we might want to work on?" Mary can see the difference. Let Mary suggest the things she wants to work on. Let the coach become a facilitator to assist Mary in improving the performance she wants to make, if any.

A perfect performance, or a "10," is simply that certain moment when, in the pursuit of excellence, the stars seem to be aligned and nothing goes wrong. Athletes have written and spoken of "the flow" or "the zone." And if it occasionally comes your way, that's great. But, wouldn't life be a whole lot more fun and less stressful if we re-set our internal bar from perfect to excellent?

I guarantee it will sure be a lot more fun for those young kids that you someday may have the privilege to coach or parent.

One last point. Be aware of perfectionists in positions of leadership. Remember, they were raised themselves by well-intended perfectionists. Because of their orientation to what's wrong, combined with feelings of being worth-less, they oftentimes are very insecure and have a great fear of failure (despite their macho facade). They tend to be great procrastinators and can stifle organizations because of their indecisiveness and inability to make major decisions (again, derived from a fear of failure).

Although the road to success is always under construction, we would all benefit from a little less criticism, the unconditional love and acceptance of our brothers and sisters, and the realization that, like snowflakes, no two people are the same.

The "one size fits all" model is simply unsustainable.

20

Accepting Personal Accountability
for Our Choices and Reactions
to External Events

For more than 20 years I had a saying that was framed on the wall in my office which read,

THERE ARE NO STRESSFUL SITUATIONS,
THERE ARE ONLY STRESSFUL RESPONSES

The word no *is used for emphasis. Yes, there are extremely tragic events that certainly demand a "stressful response." But we are talking now about everyday events that many handle with ease and lack of stress, while, others react to the identical situation with anger, resentment, jealousy, and a great deal of stress. Those who experience such stress, along with the accompanying pain and discomfort, don't realize that their choice of response or reaction is the cause of a self-inflicted wound. Those who embrace and support the adage, "There are no stressful situations, there are only stressful responses," take ownership and accountability for how they choose to respond. It doesn't mean that they don't experience anger and other negative feelings. It simply means that in being responsible for their reactions, they are more easily able to identify why they are feeling that way, and can choose to not feel stressed, and can quickly siphon off whatever thoughts were causing their distress.*

I know this sounds perverse, but many of us have known people who don't seem to be happy unless they are unhappy. Go figure. They feel victimized for their misfortune(s) and dwell on blaming others or specific events for their stress and ill feelings. Much of their "now-ness" is wasted by dwelling both mentally and emotionally on the past.

Conversely, those who accept personal accountability for the events in their lives don't waste emotional energy replaying old tapes and engaging in "would of, could of, should of" nightmares from an error in judgment, a poor choice, or misfortune.

Instead, they suck it up, still feel the pain, but quickly refocus on the present, *and quietly say to themselves, "OK, that may have been a "train wreck" but it's over! I can't change what was, but I can greatly influence what will be my present self talk and attention to the vision or picture of what I want."*

These people are very resilient. They treat setbacks as temporary. Webster defines "resiliency" as, the ability to recover quickly from illness, change, or misfortune; buoyancy.

Resilient people have great "bounce-back" capacity. They are very goal oriented and live by and practice much of what Dr. Murphy teaches. A good affirmation for dealing with setbacks is:

I treat all set backs as temporary. I am very resilient and bounce back quickly from setbacks or misfortune.

Those who live their lives accepting personal accountability for their actions move quickly to make amends for behaving in a non-loving way. They are also very forgiving people—not only of themselves but also of others.

21

How to Use Your Subconscious Mind to Remove Fear

One of our students told me that he was invited to speak at a banquet. He said he was panic-stricken at the thought of speaking before a thousand people. He overcame his fear this way: For several nights he sat down in an armchair for about five minutes and said to himself slowly, quietly, and positively, "I am going to master this fear. I am overcoming it now. I speak with poise and confidence. I am relaxed and at ease." He operated a definite law of mind and overcame his fear.

The subconscious mind is amenable to suggestion and is controlled by suggestion. When you still your mind and relax, the thoughts of your conscious mind sink down in to the subconscious through a process similar to osmosis, whereby fluids separated by a porous membrane intermingle. As these positive seeds, or thoughts, sink into the subconscious area, they grow after their kind, and you become poised, serene, and calm.

Man's greatest enemy

IT IS SAID THAT FEAR IS MAN'S GREATEST ENEMY. Fear is behind failure, sickness, and poor human relations. Millions of people are afraid of the past, the future, old age, insanity, and death. Fear is a thought in your mind, and you are afraid of your own thoughts.

Do the thing you fear
Ralph Waldo Emerson, philosopher and poet, said, "Do the thing you are afraid to do, and the death of fear is certain."

There was a time when the writer of this chapter was filled with unutterable fear when standing before an audience. The way I overcame it was to stand before the audience, do the thing I was afraid to do, and the death of fear was certain.

When you affirm positively that you are going to master your fears, and you come to a definite decision in your conscious mind, you release the power of the subconscious, which flows in response to the nature of your thought.

Fear of failure

Occasionally young people from the local university come to see me, as well as schoolteachers, who often seem to suffer from suggestive amnesia at examinations. The complaint is always the same: "I know the answers after the examination is over, but I can't remember the answers during the examination."

The idea, which realizes itself, is the one to which we invariably give concentrated attention. I find that each one is obsessed with the idea of failure. Fear is behind the temporary amnesia, and it is the cause of the whole experience.

One young medical student was the most brilliant person in his class, yet he found himself failing to answer simple questions at the time of written or oral examinations. I explained to him that the reason was that he had been worrying and was fearful for several days previous to the examination. These negative thoughts became charged with fear.

Thoughts enveloped in the powerful emotion of fear are realized in the subconscious mind. In other words, this young man was requesting his subconscious mind to see to it that he failed, and that is exactly what it did. On the day of the examination he found himself stricken with what is called, in psychological circles, suggestive amnesia.

How he overcame the fear

He learned that his subconscious mind was the storehouse of memory, and that it had a perfect record of all he had heard and read during his medical training. Moreover, he learned that the subconscious mind was responsive and reciprocal. The way to be in rapport with it was to be relaxed, peaceful, and confident.

Every night and morning he began to imagine his mother congratulating him on his wonderful record. He would hold an imaginary letter from her in his hand. As he began to contemplate the happy result, he called forth a corresponding or reciprocal response or reaction in himself. The all-wise and omnipotent power of the subconscious took over, dictated, and directed his conscious mind accordingly. He imagined the end result, thereby willing the means to the realization of that end. Following this procedure, he had no trouble passing subsequent examinations. In other words, the subjective wisdom took over, compelling him to give an excellent account of himself.

Fear of water, mountains, closed places, etc.

There are many people who are afraid to go into an elevator, climb mountains, or even swim in the water. It may well be that the individual had unpleasant experiences in the water in his youth, such as having been thrown forcibly into the water without being able to swim. He might have been forcibly detained in an elevator, which failed to function properly, causing resultant fear of closed places.

I had an experience when I was about ten years of age. I accidentally fell into a pool and went down three times. I can still remember the dark water engulfing my head, and my gasping for air until another boy pulled me out at the last moment. This experience sank into my subconscious mind, and for years I feared the water.

An elderly psychologist said to me, "Go down to the swimming pool, look at the water, and say out loud in strong tones, 'I am going to master you. I can dominate you.' Then go into the water, take lessons, and overcome it." This I did, and I mastered the water. When I assumed a new attitude of mind, the omnipotent power of the subconscious responded, giving me strength, faith, and confidence, and enabling me to overcome my fear.

Master technique for overcoming any particular fear

The following is a process and technique for overcoming fear which I teach from the platform. It works like a charm. Try it!

Suppose you are afraid of the water, a mountain, an interview, an audition, or you fear closed places. If you are afraid of swimming, begin now to sit still for five or ten minutes three or four times a day, and imagine you are swimming. Actually, you are swimming in your mind. It is a subjective experience. Mentally you have projected yourself into the water. You feel the chill of the water and the movement of your arms and legs. It is all real, vivid, and a joyous activity of the mind. It is not idle daydreaming, for you know that what you are experiencing in your imagination will be developed in your subconscious mind. Then you will be compelled to express the image and likeness of the picture you impressed on your deeper mind. This is the law of the subconscious.

You could apply the same technique if you are afraid of mountains or high places. Imagine you are climbing the mountain, feel the reality of it all, enjoy the scenery, knowing that as you continue to do this mentally, you will do it physically with ease and comfort.

Normal and abnormal fear

Man is born only with two fears, the fear of falling and the fear of loud noises. These are a sort of alarm system given you by nature as a means of self-preservation. Normal fear is good. You hear an automobile coming down the road, and you step aside to survive. The momentary fear of being run over is overcome by your action. All other fears were given to you by parents, relatives, teachers, and all those who influenced your early years.

Abnormal fear

Abnormal fear takes place when a person lets his imagination run riot. I knew a woman who was invited to go on a trip around the world by plane.

She began to cut out of the newspapers all reports of airplane catastrophes. She pictured herself going down in the ocean, being drowned, etc. This is abnormal fear. Had she persisted in this, she would undoubtedly have attracted what she feared most.

There are people who are afraid that something terrible will happen to their children, and that some dread catastrophe will befall them. When they read about an epidemic or rare disease, they live in fear that they will catch it, and some imagine they have the disease already. All this is abnormal fear.

The answer to abnormal fear

Move mentally to the opposite. To stay at the extreme of fear is stagnation plus mental and physical deterioration. When fear arises, there immediately comes with it a desire for something opposite to the thing feared. Place your attention on the thing immediately desired. Get absorbed and engrossed in your desire, knowing that the subjective always overturns the objective. This attitude will give you confidence and lift your spirits. The infinite power of your subconscious mind is moving on your behalf, and it cannot fail. Therefore, peace and assurance are yours.

He dismissed himself

The general manager of an organization told me that for three years he feared he would lose his position. He was always imagining failure. The thing he feared did not exist, save as a morbid anxious thought in his own mind. His vivid imagination dramatized the loss of his job until he became nervous and neurotic. Finally he was asked to resign.

Actually, he dismissed himself. His constant negative imagery and fear suggestions to his subconscious mind caused the latter to respond and react accordingly. It caused him to make mistakes and foolish decisions, which resulted in his failure as a general manager. His dismissal would never have happened, if he had immediately moved to the opposite in his mind.

Deliver yourself from all your fears

Learn the wonders of your subconscious, and how it works and functions. Master the techniques given to you in this chapter. Put them into practice now, today! Your subconscious will respond, and you will be free of all fears.

Step this way to freedom from fear

1. Do the thing you are afraid to do, and the death of fear is certain. Say to yourself and mean it, "I am going to master this fear," and you will.
2. Fear is a negative thought in your mind. Supplant it with a constructive thought. Confidence is greater than fear.
3. Fear is one's greatest enemy. It is behind failure, sickness, and bad human relations. Love casts out fear. Love is an emotional attachment to the good things of life. Fall in love with honesty, integrity, justice, good will, and success. Live in the joyous expectancy of the best, and invariably the best will come to you.
4. Counteract the fear suggestions with the opposite, such as "I sing beautifully; I am poised, serene, and calm." It will pay fabulous dividends.
5. Fear is behind amnesia at oral and written examination time. You can overcome this by affirming frequently, "I have a perfect memory for everything I need to know," or you can imagine a friend congratulating you on your brilliant success on the examination. Persevere and you will win.
6. You were born with only two fears, the fear of falling and the fear of loud noises. All your other fears were acquired. Get rid of them.
7. Normal fear is good. Abnormal fear is very bad and destructive. To constantly indulge in fear thoughts results in abnormal fear, obsessions, and complexes. To fear something persistently causes a sense of panic and terror.
8. You can overcome abnormal fear when you know the power of your subconscious mind can change conditions and bring to pass the cherished desires of your heart. Give your immediate attention and devo-

tion to your desire which is the opposite of your fear. This is the love that casts out fear.

9. If you are afraid of failure, give attention to success. If you are afraid of sickness, dwell on your perfect health. If you are afraid of an accident, dwell on the guidance of the Universal Mind.

10. The great law of substitution is the answer to fear. Whatever you fear has its solution in the form of your desire. If you are sick, you desire health. If you are in the prison of fear, you desire freedom. Expect the good. Mentally concentrate on the good, and know that your subconscious mind answers you always. It never fails.

11. The things you fear do not really exist except as thoughts in your mind. Thoughts are creative. Think good and good follows.

12. Look at your fears; hold them up to the light of reason. Learn to laugh at your fears. That is the best medicine.

13. Nothing can disturb you but your own thought. The suggestions, statements, or threats of other persons have no power. The power is within you. There is only one Creative Power, and It moves as harmony. There are no divisions of quarrels in it. Its source is Love.

22

Some Additional Thoughts About Fear and Its Correlation to Anger

I love Dr. Murphy's analogy in Chapter 14 of the difference in one's mental thoughts and imagination of walking across a plank on the ground and then walking across that same plank if it were raised 20 feet above the ground. Now, let's move that tension further up the fear scale and place that same plank between the rooftops of two 50-story buildings.

Ironically, walking across the plank suspended between two buildings or walking across that same plank lying on the surface of the ground require the same motor skills. But the perception of the difference in the difficulty varies substantially. On the ground level, you could skip, walk backwards and simultaneously tell a few jokes to your friends walking on the ground side by side with you.

At 50 stories above the ground, most people would probably be flat on their stomachs, carefully crawling one inch at a time. They would be equipped with a helmet, parachute, and the insistence of a safety net 50 stories below!

If we let fear overwhelm us, it can become very debilitating and a great obstacle in the accomplishment of our goals and desires.

Here are some additional thoughts following Dr. Murphy's previous chapter on "How to Use Your Subconscious Mind to Remove Fear."

I can think of few things that are more debilitating to one's progress and growth than fear. Deep fears have the capacity to totally immobilize us. So, what do we need to learn about fear, that we can better overcome it?

The first thing is the realization and understanding that fear is not a real condition but rather a combination of the thoughts and feelings we have about a condition. And since we do have the ability to control our thoughts, we have a built-in tool kit to deal with our feelings of fear. But, like any other tool kit it will not be of value to us unless we know how to use it.

Before we get to the "how to" part of this discussion, let's expand our thinking of what fear is all about. We want to examine this with a realistic, not idealistic, perspective. So, for a moment let's accept that fear is part of the human condition although from time to time we may encounter individuals who appear to be fear-less.

In looking at the word itself, consider F E A R as an acronym for,

False Expectations Appearing Real

Let's further break down the notion of fear into life threatening situations, which for the sake of this discussion we will call "real fear" and imaginary situations (all in the mind) which we will call "illusionary fear."

Most people have very few encounters with truly life threatening situations. I am talking about hiking along a trail and suddenly finding yourself between Mama bear and Baby bear. Pay attention! When confronted with a real fear situation, people tend to perform at a peak level, almost superhuman. We have heard stories of how a 120-pound mother finds her small child trapped under a car and without a moment's thought, lifts the car off the ground while someone else pulls the child to safety. The mother could have exercised and lifted weights her entire life and never have been able to lift a car without the extra adrenalin provided in this life threatening situation.

But, this is not the kind of fear that most of us experience daily, which can keep us awake at night, often resulting in some form of dis-easeness. Illusionary fear is the anticipation of something bad we think is going to happen to us, which more often than not does not occur unless we impregnate such fear thoughts so deeply in our subconscious that the fear becomes a self fulfilling prophesy. If the "bad thing" doesn't happen, it is because the person experiencing the fear discovers new data or the TRUTH of the situation, which causes their illusionary fear to dissipate. The false premise which was the basis for the thoughts and feelings of the fear become replaced with factual data, which may be completely opposite the original thoughts that first manifested in fear.

So, how is all of this going to help you deal with your own fears?

I used to think the opposite of love was hate. I then read, Love is Letting Go of Fear,* by Gerald Jampolsky, M.D. Jampolsky helped me to see things in a different light. I began to realize that hate, anger, and other such feelings all have their origin in fear. Often what is really making us angry is the fear of*

Jampolsky, Gerald, and Hugh Prather. Love is Letting Go of Fear. *Celestial Arts. 2004*

*losing something. The "something" could be losing our job, losing our part-
ner, losing the love of our children, losing our health, etc.*

*A profound presentation of the relationship between love and fear is
written in Neale Donald Walsch's book, <u>Conversations with God (Book 1)</u>**
*I believe Walsch is right on the mark. Let me share some excerpts from his
book on the subject of love and fear.*

Walsch writes,

All human actions are motivated at their deepest level by one
of two emotions—fear or love. In truth there are only two emotions—only two words in the language of the soul. These are the
opposite ends of the great polarity. . . .

Walsch continues,

"These are the two points—the Alpha and the Omega—
which allow the system you call "relativity" to be.

Without these two ideas about things, no other idea could
exist. Every human thought and every human action is based in
either love or fear. There is no other human motivation, and all
other ideas are but derivatives of these two. Every action taken by
human beings is based in love or fear, not simply those dealing
with relationships. Decisions affecting business, industry, poli-
tics, religion, the education of your young, the social agenda of
your nations, the economic goals of your society, choices involv-
ing war, peace, attack, defense, aggression, submission; determi-
nations to covet or give away, to save or to share, to unite or to
divide—every single free choice you ever undertake arises out of
one of the only two possible thoughts there are: a thought of love
or a thought of fear.

Fear is the energy which contracts, closes down, draws in,
runs, hides, hoards, harms.

Love is the energy which expands, opens up, sends out, stays,
reveals, shares, heals.

Fear wraps our bodies in clothing, love allows us to stand
naked. Fear clings to and clutches all that we have, love gives all
that we have away. Fear holds close, love holds dear. Fear grasps,
love lets go. Fear rankles, love soothes. Fear attacks, love amends.

Every human thought, word, or deed is based in one emotion
or the other. You have no choice about this, because there is noth-

*Walsch, Neale Donald. Conversations with God (Book 1). Putnam Adult. 1996.

ing else from which to choose. But you have free choice about which of these to select."

Thank you, Neale Walsch.
When I first read these words, I had the following picture in my mind:

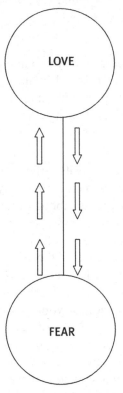

Like many people, I am a visual thinker. Words create pictures in my mind. With this illustration, I saw clearly that love and fear are at the opposite ends of a pole. And at any given time we are either experiencing love, experiencing fear, or we are moving from one pole to the other. With this realization, when I now experience feelings of fear, I know where I am in relationship to these circles. I also know where I want to be and if where I am is not where I want to be, I can make a conscious choice to take corrective action (in my thinking) and replenish my thoughts with thoughts of love and gratitude that start moving me back toward the foundation of love.

Remember the Basic Operating Principle which states, "Any thought, positive or negative, held on a continuing basis in the conscious mind, must *be brought into reality by the supraconscious mind."*

As we better understand that we create our own realities and that how we create those realities is by our thinking, the need and value of controlling our thoughts is imperative. If we cling to a fear and we keep repeating it over and over in our minds (i.e., "My business is failing," "My partner doesn't love me anymore," etc.) it must be brought into reality by the supraconscious mind.

So when we become aware of our fear(s) and how we are talking to ourselves about that fear (self talk), we have the ability to restructure, in our minds, what we are saying about the situation we believe to be causing the fear. We need to visualize a positive rather than negative picture of what we want and create a new stream of self talk that supports the end result we desire. For example, "I have all the ability in the world to build a successful business. Every day my business gets better and better," or, "I have unconditional love for my partner and every day our love for each other grows stronger and stronger."

This does not mean that businesses don't fail and people don't get divorced. As the bumper sticker reads, "Stuff Happens!"

But, people whose lives seem to continuously keep working in successful ways have either consciously or subconsciously learned the value of self talk and the reality that thought is creative.

The relevant thing about self talk in dealing with fear is the realization that we all have the power to control our thoughts. When we exert greater discipline to keep our thoughts in alignment with our values and goals, we have much greater influence over our actions and their corresponding outcomes.

If 99% of all our fears originate in thought, and we learn how to more effectively control our thoughts, then we can eradicate the compulsive fears that so often want to dominate our lives.

Now let's examine the correlation between fear and anger.

As was written earlier in this chapter, "Often what is really making us angry is the fear of losing something. The 'something' could be losing our job, losing our partner, losing the love of our children, losing our health, etc."

Consider the possibility that most anger is self directed. By that I mean most often when we experience anger, we are responding to something incomplete within us which is triggered when something or someone acts or behaves differently than how we believe it should be. For example, a child in one family might behave a certain way which angers the parent. The same behavior by a child in another family may not anger the parent at all. Or in the workplace, you might say to a fellow worker, "Doesn't it anger you when the boss keeps raising his voice?" And your fellow worker responds, "No, I find it quite amusing."

My point here is that when we are experiencing or feeling anger, we can more effectively deal with it if we understand (intellectually) that our feelings are something we have chosen rather than the result of what someone else is doing. If we accept accountability for our feelings of anger (rather than being the victim) *we have the opportunity to consider a different response to the same situation which may exclude anger. A self analysis of response(s) might be, "Why do I always get so upset when my kid leaves the front door open? Do I really want to always blow up when that happens? Is it possible that I act that way because my own father used to get so angry when I left the door open? Is there a better way I can deal with this without becoming so upset"?*

This kind of introspective questioning is healthy and can lead to a better sense of well being in addition to improved relationships.

Is being angry bad? I don't know that I would use the word bad. But I would use the word unhealthy. *Needless to say, anger has caused the demise of many relationships and there is a growing body of evidence that prolonged anger can result in ill health, including the onset of cancer.*

Laura Huxley wrote a very helpful book entitled, You Are Not the Target.* *The thrust of the book deals with the same suggestion: that most anger is self induced. When someone is acting in an angry manner toward you, it is often that you just happened to step in the cross-hairs of someone's anger that was going to be expressed anyway.*

Let me make up an example, which may cause a chuckle but, unfortunately, happens in reality far too often.

Mary has fixed a nice dinner for her husband, John, and she is looking forward to a quiet, romantic evening. John has had an unusually frustrating day at work and he is seething all the way home. When he walks in the front door, his wife greets him with a smile and says, "How was your day, darling?" John responds, "It was the worst! You ought to sit in my chair some day instead of sitting on your behind here watching television all day!"

As Laura Huxley would say, "You are not the target." Mary was feeling, "I love you, John." But John didn't even "see" Mary because he was so enraged with his boss. Mary just got in the way. It could have been his dog (who he would have probably kicked), one of his kids, or God forbid,

Huxley, Laura, You Are Not the Target. *Marlowe & Company: May, 1998 his mother-in-law. Whoever showed up first was going to get the brunt of John's stored anger.*

You may laugh at this example, but it is as undeniable as it is paradoxical that we often hurt worst those we love the most.

Consider road rage and the often insane behavior that some people express just driving their car.

A pressure cooker has a steam valve. When too much pressure builds up, the steam valve releases the pressure so the lid doesn't blow off. We can create our own steam valves by engaging in vigorous exercise, meditating, or a host of other activities that help reduce stress.

Although I have never seen a study correlating lifestyles to anger, I would guess people who eat well, exercise daily, drink moderately and get a good night's sleep have far fewer episodes of anger than people who are out of shape, overeat, and drink heavily.

Lifestyles do correlate to feelings of self esteem. Someone with a lower self image is more likely to go through life angry at the world and feeling victimized for all the bad things, relationships, etc., that have been part of their life.

Lastly, as suggested earlier, the medical field and other health practitioners are recommending to their patients the need to enhance their lifestyles and engage in activities that help alleviate stress. Exercise and diet have always been part of these recommendations, but today more and more health professions are realizing the benefits of yoga, tai chi, and meditation.

Look at the word disease. When we hyphenate it, we have dis-ease. Physical ailments and illnesses are often the effects of mental or emotional dis-easeness.

As a general guideline, it can be helpful to embrace the saying, "There are no stressful situations. There are only stressful responses."

When we accept responsibility for our choice to feel anger, we are more apt to quickly apologize and repair the damage we may have caused for our choice of how we responded to something.

So, what is the correlation between fear and anger?

Can you think of any angry response that does not contain an element of fear?

If it is road rage, is there not fear of a possible accident? If it is anger toward a spouse or loved one, may there also be a fear that she/he might leave you for another? If you are angry at your boss, might there also be a fear of losing your job?

The next time you are experiencing anger, simply say to yourself, "Time out! What is causing me to have these feelings? What am I afraid of? Do I want to continue to feel this way?" If the answer to this question is "no," change the mental picture to one that is pleasant, think of who you love and all you have to be grateful for, and deliberately leave the vibrational field of fear and start moving back toward the boundless field of love.

As John Milton wrote in his classic, Paradise Lost:

> The mind is its own place, and in itself can make a Heav'n of Hell, a Hell of Heav'n.

23

Emotional Mastery: Common Sense Steps for Total Life Transformation

by Lee Pulos, Ph.D., ABPP

One of the greatest myths that still pervades mind/body medicine is that stress is the primary villain and cause of most of our problems. Stress provides a simple explanation for why we are sick, depressed, bored, alcoholic or burnt out. Stress as a possible precipitating factor in disease cannot be dismissed as unimportant, but neither can it be cited as the cause of all of our dysfunction.

There are countless examples where stress has been cited as the cause of death. There are numerous situations that have been documented of people being overwhelmed by stressful events and suddenly dying. For instance, King Phillip V of Spain dropped dead when he learned of a great Spanish defeat. The Roman Emperor Neva died in a fit of anger, evidently at a senator who offended him.

More recently, the wife of the owner of the motel where Martin Luther King was assassinated suffered a stroke a few hours later and died soon thereafter. Lyndon Johnson, who had said that when the Great Society died he would die, succumbed to a heart attack the day after the Nixon administration announced a complete dismantling of the former president's programs. And the list goes on.

In all of these examples, the stressful event, rather than how the person viewed it, came to be identified as the critical factor, leaving the erroneous impression that what happens to us is more important than how we perceive it. Which goes back to a quote from William Osler, the great 19th century physician said to be the father of modern medicine, "It is not the disease the patient has that is important—but more important the patient who has the disease."

The stress-and-sickness legend has continued to grow to the point that stress has become the 21st century scapegoat for our problems. Yet, there is considerable evidence that shows many people stay healthy under both everyday stress and extreme stress-producing circumstances.

Hippocrates, the Greek physician stated, "Whatever happens in the mind influences the body and vice versa." In other words, the body and mind are one and each is continuously influencing the other. Thoughts, beliefs and imagination are not just abstracting from the mind but electro-chemical events with physiological consequences.

In his book *The New Brain*,* neurologist Dr. Richard Restak has pointed out that there has been an almost exponential increase in Attention Deficit Disorder (ADD) and Attention Deficit Hyperactivity Disorder (ADHD) in children in the past ten to fifteen years. While there are several reasons for this alarming increase, a recurring theme is the significant escalation of multi-tasking of faxing, emails, texting, tweeting, music videos which flash eight to one hundred images a minute, cell phones, frequent exposure to graphic scenes of violence, laptop computers, the internet and the list goes on. The modern age is rewiring our brains. Some of the symptoms of ADD are chronic procrastination, a sense of underachievement, many projects going on simultaneously, trouble following through, easily distractible, impulsive and low tolerance for frustration, chronic problems with self-esteem–and there are at least eleven additional symptoms. There are now six different kinds of ADD which can be managed with medication, neurofeedback training or Emotional Freedom Technique (EFT) which I will describe in more detail later.

In a recent study, psychologist Dr. Betsy Sparrow of Columbia University reported that Google is altering our brain. When we know where to find information, we are less likely to remember it—an amnesia called "The Google Effect." Her study was published in *Science* and sug-

*Restak, Richard. The New Brain: How the Modern Age is Rewiring Your Mind. *Rodale Books. 2003*

gests that human memory is reorganizing where it goes for information, adapting to new technologies rather than relying on pure memory. In other words, people are better at remembering where to find facts rather than the facts themselves.

In another study, workplace stress was described as an epidemic. In the same article, it was pointed out that one third of all heart attacks occur between 7am and 9 am on Monday mornings and 80 percent of strokes in men occur between 8 am and noon on Mondays. The study, of 600 American workers, was conducted by the Northwestern National Life Insurance Company. Additional findings included that one in seven workers quit their job because the stress was too great for them to handle and another one third will seriously consider quitting their jobs due to job stress. In addition, three of four workers "regularly" experience some sort of stress-caused illness such as exhaustion or burnout, anxiety, muscle pains and headaches.

Meanwhile, the American Institute of Stress estimates that between 75 percent and 90 percent of all doctors' visits are caused by reactions to stress.

Stanford University neuroscientist Robert Sampolsky has researched and written extensively how sustained stress releases adrenaline and cortisone, stress hormones which can cause between 12% and 15% reduction in the hippocampi, which are the major memory relay stations in the emotional limbic system. This explains why persons with post-traumatic stress from accidents or combat have significant problems with short-term memory and recall. One of my clients, a Type A driven executive with very high stress levels described having a "Swiss cheese memory."

I taught him how to do EFT, which works by stimulating key acupoints in the electrical or energetic anatomy of the body and he was very impressed in that we reduced his stress level on a ten point scale from a nine to a one by the end of the hour. He called me three days later to say that he is no longer "gasp" breathing, the tension's "almost gone" in his body and he was able to sleep through the night.

The good news is that the brain is very malleable, and the neuroplasticity of the brain can regain normal functions once stress and anxiety levels are reduced along with a change in lifestyle.

Although many people use the term "stressed out" to describe how they feel, most are not aware of the circumstances that are actually causing the stress. They see their stress as the result of helplessness or powerlessness in controlling certain aspects of their lives. Sometimes it is related to a demanding job or as part of a family or relationship issue. Most people are too busy to think about why they feel the way they do—a stress symptom itself.

Of course, this leads to sleeplessness as one goes to bed trying to deal with challenges by obsessing over and over with negative self-talk. Another symptom is the inability to control anger, which can be related to unfulfilled perfectionism, which is driven by the fear of failure rather than a desire to succeed. People who lack assertiveness or are pleasers frequently give their power away to others rather than defining themselves and their needs. Of course uncertainty, fear, and self doubt all reinforce a lack of self-esteem which becomes a self-defeating downward spiral.

Psychologist Dr. Judith Rodin has spent much of her career researching the importance of control. She states that feelings of control and self-determination are of central importance in influencing psychological and physical health and perhaps even longevity in older adults.

Dr. Rodin and her colleagues measured stress-related hormones in several groups of nursing home residents and then taught the residents coping skills to help them deal better with day-to-day stresses. They were taught to say no when they didn't want to do things without worrying that they were going to offend other people. The residents were also taught assertiveness training and time management skills.

After the training, these people had significantly reduced blood levels of cortisol, a hormone closely associated with stress that has been implicated in a variety of diseases. Moreover, cortisol levels among the "assertiveness trained" people remained lower even after 18 months. In addition, these people were much healthier and had a greatly reduced need for medication compared with those who had not been taught coping skills.

Control, or lack of it, is also related to our ability to fight off disease. Our immune system is the "defense" system of the body. However, when we feel "defenseless" with little sense of control, our defense system is compromised. Dr. Rodin established that people who experience the most uncontrollable events had suppressed immune systems and experienced more infections and other diseases.

While waking hypnosis or self-talk may explain how we empower or limit ourselves in our journey through life, what else can we do to strengthen our inner core and self-esteem?

One of the recurring themes I see in many of my clients is that they are conflict-phobic and will do almost anything to avoid expressing negative emotions or standing up for themselves. The problem is that whatever negative emotions one "stuffs" over and over will eventually end up "stuffing" them. That is, unexpressed emotions in the course of time will find a parking place somewhere in the body. This is one of the cornerstones of psychosomatic conditions and as one of my medical friends tells her patients, "The body is crystallized thought. What emotions are you avoiding that are now manifesting in that part of your body?"

One of my clients complained of harboring considerable anger toward her husband who was overbearing and controlling, but she didn't know how to express herself or deal with him. After considerable discussion, I suggested she express herself in the following manner: "I have something to say to you that may be hurtful, but my intention is not to hurt you but to strengthen our relationship. Would this be a good time to let you know what I am feeling?" She said that for the first time he listened to her, acknowledged her feelings, and agreed to make some changes as their relationship was starting to fray at the edges.

The point being that the more transparent and emotionally honest one can be with their feelings, the greater their psychological and physical health. As one avoids or diminishes the expression of resentment or anger, the more they are diluting their expression of love. The more emotionally honest one is with the expression of anger, with harm to none, the more expansive and deepening will be their expression of love.

In my work with couples, following the history taking, I will have them take turns emptying their "gunnysack of grievances" that has filled up over the years. The only ground rule is that the person hearing or receiving the cumulated grievances cannot defend themselves. Once both "gunnysacks" have been emptied, they cannot go back and keep reminding their partner of their mistakes or wrongdoings or sins that may have happened years ago. From there, each partner makes a simple demand for the change that would strengthen or improve the relationship that is agreed upon by both persons.

This is a wonderful communication tool that encourages emotional honesty, transparency and an opportunity to be forthcoming and assertive, especially if one is conflict-phobic and fearful of standing up for themselves. This technique also creates a sense of equality even though one partner may tend to be more domineering or controlling. As one of my clients said following the session, "I no longer feel like the bottom dog. My husband had to listen to me and understand my frustrations. I feel much closer to him now."

Thus, it is important to create mental antibodies to neutralize toxic thoughts. When you catch yourself drugging your mind with "bad hypnosis" or negative self-talk, constructively ask yourself why you are doing so? "Why am I planting weeds in the garden of my subconscious and watering the weeds all day long instead of flowers?"

Since we are all striving for optimal health, symptoms are a message from the subconscious that we need to change something in our lives. If you have a physical symptom, do not run away from it. Feel its reality in your body. Let the associated emotions flow freely. If you allow them to flow almost as if you are free associating, they will lead you to the root cause or beliefs that are creating the physical symptom.

Our psychic fault lines are rumbling and the tectonic plates of consciousness are shifting. While most of us may not have the important tools or insight to create emotional mastery and optimal health, in their book, *The Life We Are Given,** Michael Murphy and George Leonard describe one of the best programs I am aware of for creating and maintaining the highest level of mental, emotional and physical health. The main theme of their program is that any long-term change requires on-going practice, not a fast-fix seminar.

* *Murphy, Michael, and George Leonard.* The Life We Are Given: A Long-term Program for Realizing the Potential of Body, Mind, Heart and Soul. *G.P. Putnam's Sons. 1995.*

Implicit in their program is that each of us has hidden human reserves or potential that has yet to be discovered. Secondly, change must be expansive and involve not only body and mind but heart and soul.

The integrated practice created by Murphy and Leonard was designed for people with busy lives. It includes the following commitments:

1. To establish a clear goal, a physical or mental achievement of positive human potential.
2. To create and utilize belief statements or affirmations daily for significant positive change. All of the participants shared one affirmation; "My entire being is balanced, vital and healthy," in addition to individual specific affirmations.
3. To establish a Kata or physical action such as yoga, Qi Gong or Tai Qi that involves some stretching and strength exercises.
4. Every Kata ends with ten minutes of meditation and visualization.
5. Each person selected a specific part of their body or mind they wanted to heal.
6. Develop intellectual power by reading, writing and discussion.
7. Becoming conscious of everything one eats but emphasizing the benefits of low fat and high fiber foods.
8. Whenever possible, to open your heart to others in love and service, but also to nurture your own emotional needs.

Three things were crucial to one's personal growth. First, a clear vision of the goal that was to be achieved. Second, the daily affirmations that reinforced ongoing change, and third, the Kata or ongoing physical training for both the body and mind, followed by meditation and visualization.

Some of the results reported by the participants in this project were truly extraordinary and bordered on the miraculous. A woman developed cataracts at the age of forty-two. Her father went blind from cataracts and this appeared to be a family condition. Two years after the diagnosis and increasing growth of her cataracts, which began to diminish her vision, she joined the Murphy and Leonard program which met every Saturday morning for two hours. The affirmation she chose was, "My eyes are free of cataracts and growing stronger daily." Her doctor said, "Your eyes will never improve," so she changed doctors. While doing her Kata or physical exercise, she decided her affirmation should be more specific, "My lenses are free of cataracts." In addition, she would make energy passes over her eyes to move healing energy to the cataracts. She would also visualize water squirting over the lenses or the lenses cleaning themselves. A year later she went for prescription sunglasses and the doctor said that her left eye was totally clear and healthy and her right eye had a very small, hardly noticeable deposit but not big enough to be called a cataract.

The key to this extraordinary success is that sustained and focused practice, rather than talent, is the key to peak performance in any field. Murphy and Leonard provide a number of inspirational examples of success in their book. Their rule of thumb, however, is "mentors yes, gurus no." In other words, don't give your power away to gurus, who in many cases foster dependency, but to use mentors and your own power to create the most healthy, joyous and brilliant future possible.

One of life's little puzzles is why some people tend to sail through life with few or no illnesses while others succumb to every bug they encounter? In a fascinating book, *The Immune Power Personality,** author Henry Dreher argues that longevity and health are characterized by seven personality traits. Healthy people are:

1. Attuned to their mind-body signals of pleasure and pain, including such things as fatigue, anger and sadness.
2. Have the confidence and ability to confide their secrets, traumas and feelings to others instead of "stuffing" and keeping things locked inside.
3. They exhibit the three C's: a sense of control over their health and quality of life, a strong commitment to work and relationships, and an ability to see stress as a challenge rather than a threat.
4. Are appropriately assertive about their needs and feelings.
5. Tend to form relationships based on unconditional love rather than frustrated power.
6. Are altruistically committed to helping others and being of service.
7. Demonstrate a willingness to be emotionally honest in exploring the many different facets of their personalities, good and bad, looking for the inner strengths to fall back on in case of challenges or failures.

*Dreher, Henry. The Immune Power Personality. A Dutton Book. 1995

While not everyone can immediately shift into a new way of thinking and being, with awareness comes choice and commitment. Emotional
mastery involves the decision to begin reinventing ourselves at one's own
speed and style for long-term gains, happiness and health.

When Dr. Joseph Murphy wrote the first edition of his book nearly
fifty years ago, aside from hypnosis and medications, there was very little
to offer people who were suffering from stress, phobias, trauma, performance anxiety or depression. Twenty-five years ago, however, psychologist Dr. Roger Callahan developed a technique based on acupuncture theory and treatment processes that emerged from applied and educational
kinesiology that he labeled Thought Field Therapy, or TFT. His treatment
process evolved into Emotional Freedom Technique, or EFT which is
based more or less on the same theoretical thinking as TFT but is easier to
learn and is just as effective.

I have utilized both TFT and EFT for almost twenty years and teach
it to most of my clients in our first session. That way, the client can begin
utilizing EFT on their own at home, and once the technique is mastered,
one can treat themselves in under two minutes.

EFT works with our energetic anatomy. For over four thousand years,
insights into our energetic anatomy have emerged from both China and
India who have shared the knowledge that there are energetic rivers or
pathways along which our vital force, our life energy, flows through our
bodies. These could be thought of as similar or analogous to the unseen
network of underground streams in the earth.

In Asian medicine, these pathways are called "meridians" and are energetic streams that flow through twelve meridians and form the basis
for acupuncture and EFT. They contain the acupressure points that will
be stimulated for treatment. Chinese physicists and German doctors have
established that meridians emit light and can actually be seen with infra-
red photography. Researchers have found that with stress, fear, or illness,
less light or energy is emitted from the meridians and acupoints and that
acupuncture, or with EFT, tapping or rubbing certain points increases the
amount of light released or emitted.

There are twelve meridians in the body that travel to twelve different organs and energize twelve separate sets of muscle groups. In addi-

tion, there are two carrier meridians, one in which yin or sedating energy flows, and yang or energizing energy is transported by the second carrier meridian.

There will be two simple set-up procedures that will be done prior to the tapping or rubbing the twelve treatment acupoints on the head, body and fingers. Of importance, each meridian or treatment point has an emotion that is associated with it. For example, the emotions for the bladder meridian are trauma and fear, for the gall bladder meridian rage, for the stomach meridian stress and anxiety, and so on.

Also of importance, while doing the treatment you must focus on the problem or issue. While that may seem counter-intuitive, I ask my clients to think of themselves as a violin. If their issue is anxiety, metaphorically, the first string of the violin is out of tune, or sour notes, representing their anxiety. As they focus on their issue while stimulating the twelve acupoints in sequence, the tapping of the points triggers the brain to release beta endorphins which are the body's natural morphine molecules and are twenty-seven times more powerful than synthetic morphine. What else releases beta endorphins? Exercise, laughter, good music, sex, acupuncture, and of course, EFT.

For example, I recently saw a young woman who was referred to me because she was suffering from moderate PTSD following a serious motor vehicle accident. We were able to "re-tune" the first violin string from an eight to a one on a ten point scale, which significantly reduced her fear and unease about driving. However, she said, "Something still doesn't' feel right." As we explored a little further, it turned out there were two more symbolic violin strings that were out of tune. The first, driving at night in the rain and second, taking a left turn which is how she got t-boned, almost totaling her car. We did EFT for both the "new" dissonant violin strings, reducing all three strings to a one and she broke out into a big smile and remarked, "I can breathe now. I don't feel like having a panic attach or terrified to think about driving in the rain or turning left."

As you go through stimulating the sequence of acupoints, most people find that two, three or four acupoints feel especially relaxing. I suggest that you spend more time stimulating those points as the emotions associated with those meridians will have more relevance to your issue.

Following the reduction of fear, stress or depression to a SUD (or subjective units of distress) of one, you will then install a positive affirmation to support the more empowering belief. As an example, if your issue was stress or anxiety, you will stimulate each acupoint of the head and body in sequence while repeating, an affirmation such as, "I am confident, calm and relaxed."

Once you do the procedure on yourself two or three times, it will be very easy to memorize the sequence so in the future you will be able to complete the complete order of acupoints in under two minutes.

The complete step-by-step set-up, treatment sequence and installations of positive affirmations will be provided in the appendix of this book along with detailed graphics to help you identify the acupoints on your head, body and hands.

EFT has revolutionized the way many practitioners deal with trauma, simple and complex phobias, panic attacks, addictions, depression, anger, stress and generalized anxiety, pain and sleep dysfunction. There are now 70,000 EFT practitioners in fifty-five countries.

With a little bit of practice and review of the EFT protocol in the appendix, you will be adding a new dimension of control and emotional mastery to your life. I wish you well on your journey to an optimal and brilliant future.

Key 7

RELEASE YOUR FULL POTENTIAL

Understanding who we REALLY
are and the need to dispose
of our "Mental Garbage" on a
daily basis.

24

Moving On . . . An Invitation to the Path of Enlightenment

In the pursuit of knowledge,
something is added every day.
In the pursuit of enlightenment,
something is dropped every day.

Lao-tzu

So, what have we learned? We should have a clear understanding of the three areas of the mind (conscious, subconscious, and supraconscious) and how they interact with each other.

1. *The **subconscious** is our "hard drive" in which all learning, experiences and the feelings associated with such are stored. It is constantly at work carrying out the instructions given to it by the conscious mind, for better or for worse. It is non-judgmental and proceeds to help facilitate the wishes and commands from the conscious mind. It also monitors and manages all of our bodily functions.*

2. *The **conscious** mind is the traffic cop. It determines what is good or bad, right or wrong (not always the TRUTH, but rather its perception of the truth based on prior data and experiences stored in the subconscious). It directs us to move toward those events and situations that will bring us comfort and make us feel good, and avoid those situations which may create discomfort (i.e., moving toward pleasure and avoiding pain).*

3. *The **supraconscious** is our source of all pure creativity and provides the conscious area of the mind access to all data or information not otherwise stored in our subconscious memory bank. It also provides excess free-flowing energy when we are constructively motivated.*

It is important to understand that consciousness creates matter and form. Matter does not create consciousness. The book, Kindle, I-Pad or how-

ever you are reading these pages was created by conscious thought, just as were the words written. The chair you are sitting in or the bed you are lying on was created through consciousness. Look around the room you are in and realize that everything you see was created through conscious intent.

So, we have been given this incredible gift of creativity. We truly create our own reality through our conscious intent. Now that we know how this works and have the tools to create whatever we want, (see Chapter 8, "Affirmations and Affirmation Techniques"), we can begin to eliminate the false beliefs and erroneous data we have carried with us for too long and that no longer serve us well.

And, to Enlightenment.

I would like to end this book by sharing with you a paper I wrote on Enlightenment on my birthday in 2001. Some of what is written is redundant to what you have already read in this book. I considered editing it out, but felt it took away from the subject of Enlightenment. And, repetition is a great aid in learning, so here we go:

ON ENLIGHTENMENT
(February 21, 2001)

The 70's! Wow, what an exciting decade.

Before I speak on enlightenment, let me provide a historical perspective for those of you who had not yet reached adulthood by the 1970's.

I doubt in recent history there was any twenty-year span of greater social evolution than the twenty year period from the mid 1950's to the mid 1970's.

In the 1950's most American marriages were what we thought of then as "traditional," with the husband being the economic provider and the wife the homemaker and dominant parent. A significant percentage of marriages were accelerated by loving or enthusiastic sex resulting in an unplanned pregnancy. (There was no Pill!)

A young couple in love would often choose marriage just so they could live together. Living together out of wedlock in the 1950's was truly scandalous and unaccepted by society.

The term "women's liberation" had not yet been coined and Ralph Nader was still in school, thus the birth of consumerism was in incubation. There was no active gay movement.

So, imagine the pent-up personal and social tensions that, given any opportunity, had to inevitably erupt.

A significant catalyst to what became a social revolution was the invention and emergence of the Pill. This takes us to the 1960's. Young couples (or people of any age) could fully have sex, no longer fearing an unplanned or unexpected pregnancy. By the mid to late 60's, society became accepting of a couple's choice to live together without the blessing of the church.

Another huge influence in bringing about this radical social change was the Vietnam War.

The Vietnam War was the first war brought into the living room in full color. It was not unusual for a family, following dinner, to watch TV in horror. And for what, was the prevailing question. Student protests against the military draft were common, and then there was Kent State.

By the end of the '60s, the Beatles were in full force, "Hair" was the number one Broadway musical, marijuana had worked its way from college campuses to the workplace, women had burned countless bras, and Women's Lib was a real deal. Ralph Nader had brought consumer rights public, gays and lesbians were coming out of the closet daily, and Maharishi Mahesh Yogi had brought Transcendental Meditation to the West.

Imagine all of that happening in just twenty short years. People were finally being allowed to align their behavior and activities with their true selves.

The human development movement was well launched with a outpouring of self-help books, seminars, and experimental social drugs. More and more people were introspectively asking the questions, "Why am I here? What's this all about? What is my purpose in life?"

In 1975 a friend had given me a copy of Tim Gallwey's new best seller, The Inner Game of Tennis. *I remember reading the book on a flight from Los Angeles to Portland. I was incredibly inspired by Tim's use of tennis as simply a metaphor for the inner game of life with its focus on performance.*

Upon my arrival home, I picked up the telephone and began calling names or institutions mentioned in his book in an attempt to locate Tim. After probably ten phone calls, I finally reached Tim at his home in Malibu, California. My first words were, "Tim, you don't know me, but I know you because I just read your book. I would like to invite you to come to Portland as my guest (and for a fee) to speak with our employees." And he did.

Tim is one of the clearest thinkers I have ever met. He seemed to have a profound answer for any question I would ask, regardless of the subject. I used to think that no human being could have possibly learned that much and that somehow Tim had opened certain channels to receive knowledge beyond what he personally "knew."

After some time and many get-togethers, I asked Tim the question, "Tim, what is enlightenment?" (Remember, on Broadway, "Hair" was singing that this was the dawning of the Age of Aquarius, the word "enlightenment" was working its way into our culture, and Shirley MacLaine was to take us Out On a Limb.)

So, to enlightenment.

I don't remember Tim's exact words, but I do believe I remember his meaning (so forgive me, Tim, if I take a little editorial license here).

The essence of what I heard was that enlightenment becomes a process where we begin to discover that everything we have always thought we wanted to be, we already are. And, wrapped up in this piece of skin we call "us" already exists total love, total truth, wisdom, knowledge, intelligence, beauty, etc., etc. But, to become more of that, which in truth we already are, requires an ability to become less of that which we think we are.

For the truly enlightened individual, therefore, growth becomes a process of subtraction. Most of us have been trained to believe that growth is a process of addition. We become addicted to adding on. Better car, bigger house, more toys, etc., etc.

Tim implied that real growth occurs when we begin to unlearn or take away those things that are interfering with our ability to express that which in truth we already are. I believe much of what Tim meant by what we have to eliminate are beliefs, attitudes and outdated ways of viewing the world that simply no longer serve us well.

When we first arrived in this world, we were like an empty vessel. We had no opinions, attitudes, beliefs, or prejudices about anything. I think this is part of the fascination that attracts us to infants and small children. We are almost reverent of their innocence and belief that nothing is impossible.

Parents, teachers, coaches, and others we admire as small children also have significant impact and influence on shaping us to become who we think we are. It is the "who we think we are," our persona or description of ourself to others, that causes us to act consistently in accordance with that description. Most of us go through life not understanding or realizing that this description (or self image) is no different than a costume. But, we mistakenly come to believe the costume is the real us. Therefore, we never consider changing it or taking it off. We simply say, "That's the way I am. I always _____ (fill in the blank)."

It is only when we come to the realization that our true self is oftentimes radically different than our perception of our self that we can begin to grow. And once again, the growth becomes the process of subtracting the myths and often false beliefs that heretofore hindered our growth and development. We finally come to see the difference between the Truth and our perception of the "truth" as error.

This realization brings with it great empowerment and liberation. The enlightened individual becomes fully accountable for his or her actions and no longer plays the role *of the victim of destiny.*

This is enlightenment.

Lastly, knowing this Truth and being this Truth are not always the same. We put a lot of time and effort into the making of our costume and old habits are sometimes hard to change. But, it does become easier once we learn how that costume was created and we clearly understand that it is *a costume.*

In conclusion, having information about a subject, in this case enlightenment, doesn't prove that the person speaking or writing on enlightenment is necessarily enlightened. It has been said we teach that which we need to learn the most.

As I say about my relationship with God: God is always with me, but I may not always be with God.

Thank you for joining Dr. Murphy and me on this journey. You really **are** *terrific just the way you are. Accept your magnificence.*

Visualize a tug boat plowing through the water with great effort towing a barge full of garbage. Think of the barge as your "excess baggage." Think of the barge housing all of the "garbage" you have collected along the way that is no longer relevant to how you choose to live your life today. In our homes we throw out the garbage daily. Why not do the same thing with your own mind? And now you know how.

All we have to do is cut the line towing the garbage and freeing up the energy of the tug boat (ourselves) that can now joyfully cruise through the waters of life relieved of the burden of towing unnecessary weight.

Much love to you all and the better world we all have the capacity to co-create as our own legacy and gift to our children's and grandchildren's generations.

The artist does not identify with the colors he uses. He knows he chooses them, and applies them with a brush. So you paint your reality with your ideas in the same manner. You are not your ideas nor even your thoughts. You are the self who experiences them. If a painter finds his hands stained with pigment at the end of the day, he can wash the stain off easily, knowing its nature. If you think that limiting thoughts are a portion of you, permanently attached therefore, you will not think of washing them off.

The Nature of Personal Reality* by Jane Roberts

*Roberts, Op. cit., p. 13

Appendix A

An Affirmation Workshop

One of the great take-home values intended from the reading of this book is for the reader to more fully understand the power of his/her own self talk (Chapter 3), and how the subconscious is forever present, always available to carry out the "commands" given to it by the conscious area of the mind. Now that we more fully understand that the subconscious does not question the value of our "commands," but just proceeds to fulfill such "instructions," we will find ourselves more consciously aware of how we are talking to ourselves and what we are saying.

We may want to "cancel" certain thoughts or statements often said in frustration and substitute the language consistent with the picture we want to create.

For example: "How can I be so stupid to not check my calendar and be late for another meeting! Damn, I seem to do that all the time!"

Whoa!! Is that what we want to be commanding to our subconscious mind when our goal is to become more and more orderly and punctual? Of course not. So, if we find ourselves making such a statement in anger or frustration, we simply put our record button on "pause." We then take a couple of deep breathes and say "Cancel," and we visually see ourselves erasing the negative statement we just made.

Two more breathes and with a smile in our heart we say to ourselves: "Every day and in every way I am becoming more and more orderly and punctual. My calendar is a great tool to ensure that I am always on time for my meetings. I feel good about the fact I am always *orderly and punctual."*

You must choose to repeat this 2–3 times. We want to totally *erase (or cancel) the negative statement and leave the subconscious with a clear picture of the "new me" who "feels good about the* fact *I am always orderly and punctual."*

In Chapter 8, "Affirmations and Affirmation Techniques," I mentioned that I was initially skeptical that by just saying certain words to ourselves we could bring about positive changes in our behavior. I also said the greatest testimony to the effectiveness of affirmations came from the class students themselves who had been through the seminar previously and were taking a refresher course. John Boyle affectionately referred to these class partici-pants as "re-treads." But, their real life testimonials of the positive changes, healings, growth in relationships, family dynamics, sports performance, business success, etc., etc., seemed endless and most credible supporting their success from having incorporated the daily practice of affirmations into their lives.

Remember that affirmations are powerful tools to help you achieve your goals. It is best to write down your goals and then prioritize them in their im-portance to you. It is also best to have no more than 15 goals at any one time. As you achieve each goal, one at a time, you can always add the next goal.

Let me also add that it is very important that we build balance into our goal setting. We have all seen individuals who so heavily drive themselves to succeed in business, for example, only to find that family relationships and personal health may suffer in the process.

Balance is essential. Think of the individual pie sections in the circle be-low as the most important aspects of your life. As you fill in each section, you might end up with something like this:

Balance Wheel of Life

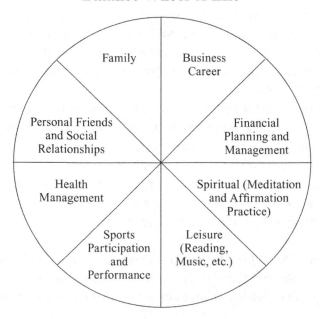

These are just examples. The key is for you to determine the most important things in your life. This will vary from person to person.

Once you have your goals <u>clearly</u> defined, you want to create a mental picture of what the accomplishment of those goals would look like in your own life. Important: you do not create a picture that is limited by who you know or don't know, how much money you have or don't have, but rather you play a game of "make believe" by creating the pictures that match up with your goals in a perfect world. Because what you will discover is that it is a perfect world and we truly have the capacity to "make beliefs" come true when we fully utilize the God-given tools that we have always had that may just need a little sharpening and the removal of some rust that may have occurred during periods of inactivity.

So, we form a clear picture of a goal we have and what it will look like, in detail, when we manifest the reality of that picture into our daily lives. We then create the words to support the picture (goal) as though it were true today, i.e.,

"I look good and feel good at _____ pounds."
"I eat only enough to maintain my perfect weight of ___ pounds."
"I enjoy the benefits of exercising every day and never miss a day."

And as I make these statements (affirmations) to myself (the words), I see the end result (the picture) in my mind as though it were true today, and I feel good (the emotion) that, "I look good and feel good at _____ pounds."

Important: as stated earlier in this book, the purpose of language is to create or access an image. It is not the words that record in our subconscious, but the pictures our words create along with the feelings or emotions associated with those pictures.

Now let me share with you six affirmations that have brought about substantial improvements in the lives of many. It is also recommended if this is your first use of affirmations, that you just use the following six affirmations for the first 30 days before adding additional affirmations.

1. *"I like (love) myself unconditionally."*
    This is a link to all other goals. It is an affirmation you should fully expect to use for the rest of your life. It is an affirmation that continues to build high self esteem. We cannot give more love to another than that which we have for ourself.

With small children it is good to teach them to say, "I like myself."
Over time this transforms to, "I love myself," which then transforms to,
"Now that I love myself, I find that I love everyone."

2. "I never devalue myself through destructive self-criticism."
    It makes no sense to use affirmation #1, "I like myself," if we keep beat-
    ing ourselves up with demeaning and destructive self-criticism.
    Some people with low self esteem simply find it easier to accept
    a criticism than a compliment. To them I might say, "What if your best
    friend talked to you all day long about you the way you talk about
    yourself all day? Would you like to hang out with that person? Of
    course not."
    Immediately cease all destructive self-criticism.
    "I never devalue myself (or others) through destructive self-criticism."

3. "I have unconditional warm regards for all people at all times."
    (The exception to this is a psychopath who both legally and clinically
    doesn't know right from wrong)
    The affirmation, "I have unconditional warm regards for all people
    at all times," is designed to create superior human relations. This is a
    wonderful trait to have. People who embrace this tenet focus on the es-
    sence (goodness) of the individual, which sometimes may be in conflict
    with that person's behavior. As we wrote in Chapter 19, criticize the deed,
    not the doer. A parent might say to his child, "I love you, Johnny/Mary,
    but I don't love what you did. You are much better than that, and we do
    not expect you to do that (the behavior) again." The intention here is to
    criticize the deed but leave the doer's self esteem intact.
    Lastly, people who have warm regards also have great empathy.
    They realize that everyone has had a different life journey and the vari-
    ance of such journeys can cause people to act (re-act) radically different
    to often the same situation.
    An old Cheyenne proverb reads: "Before you take off on another per-
    son, walk a mile in his moccasins."
    "I have unconditional warm regards for all people at all times."

4. "I am easily able to relax at any time and every day through every affirma-
    tion, I become healthier in both mind and body."
    There is a growing body of scientific evidence that so many health prob-
    lems are related to tension, stress, and our inability to relax. In a rapidly
    growing technology and information world, it seems like someone keeps
    turning up the speed on the treadmill. We run faster but don't seem to
    run further.

We need to proactively manage the stress in our lives. The word dis-ease itself, when hyphenated, is dis-ease. If we let stress accumulate and don't have healthy outlets to allow it to siphon off, i.e., exercise, medita-tion, et.al., we may subject ourselves to physical dis-easeness.

Please re-read Marilyn's Schlitz's introductory paragraph to Chapter 11, "Mental Healings in Modern Times." Affirmation #4 is a proactive step to remind ourselves of our need to relax and create balance in our lives.

5. "I am completely self-determined and allow others the same right."
Most of us don't have a problem with the first half of this affirmation, but may put up a little resistance when our business partner, spouse, or others exert their right to do the same.

"I am completely self-determined and allow <u>others</u> the same right."

6. "I am completely responsible for all of my responses to all other persons and to all events."
This is so important that we devoted an entire chapter in this book to this subject (see Chapter 20, "Accepting Personal Accountability for Our Choices and Reactions to External Events").

Begin using these six affirmations now, and only these affirmations, for the next 30 days. People will say to you, "What are you doing. You are different!" And, they mean this in a positive, constructive manner.

Summary:

Affirmations, when properly directed, are incredibly powerful tools in our lives. Please re-read Chapter 8, "Affirmations and Affirmation Techniques." Since we discuss in detail the best time of day to do your affirmations and other helpful hints, I won't repeat those here.

I hope this Appendix has been helpful to you in expanding your under-standing and application of the use of affirmations.

Namaste

Appendix B

Dr. Pulos—Adventures in Learning

Emotional Freedom Technique (EFT) Treatment Protocol

The *primary purpose of EFT* is to release any blockage in the meridian system or the electrical circulatory system of the body.

STEP 1   On a 1–10 point scale, EFT works best when the anxiety, fear or your issue is greater than 5–6

STEP 2   Begin the treatment by correcting for neurological disorganization (see attached diagram and description of terms). Place three fingers in your belly button and with the thumb and ring finger of your other hand rub the collarbone points (Kidney 27) for ten seconds.

        Kidney 27—Down one inch from the sternal notch and two inches out from midline until you feel a small indentation that is often tender.

STEP 3   *Rub the Neurolymphatic Reflex* (tender spot above the heart) for 5–7 seconds. (Metaphorically, think of this as putting a new fuse in the fuse box of your body.)

STEP 3a   While rubbing the "tender area," you may wish to say the following forgiveness (Optional) affirmations to yourself:
    a) Even though I have this anxiety/fear/issue, I deeply and completely accept myself.
    b) Even though I have this anxiety/fear/issue, I deeply and completely forgive myself for anything I might have done to contribute to it.
    c) Even though I have this anxiety/fear/issue, I completely accept and forgive myself and anyone else who may have contributed to it.

Note: "All healing has to go through the door of forgiveness."
                                              —Dr. Caroline Myss

STEP 4   While focusing on your fear/anxiety/issue (i.e., focusing on the violin string that is "out of tune"), either rub or tap the following acupuncture points for 7–10 seconds.

	Location	Meridian	Emotion
1.	Beginning of eyebrows	Bladder 2	Trauma, Frustration
2.	1/2 inch from outer corners of eyes	Gall Bladder 1	Rage, Fury
3.	Under the eyes (Below the pupil, touching Below the orbital bone)	Stomach 1	Anxiety, Stress
4.	Under nose	Governing Vessel 26	Embarrassment
5.	Under lip	Conception Vessel 24	Shame
6.	Collarbone	Kidney 27	Fear
7.	Under the arm (4-inches below armpit)	Spleen 21	Anxiety about the future & security
8.	Inside corner of thumb-nail	Lung 11	Contempt, Intolerance
9.	Inside corner of index fingernail	Large Intestine 1	Guilt, Sadness, Grief
10.	Inside corner of middle fingernail	Triple Warmer 9	Regret, Jealousy, Sexual Tension
11.	Inside corner of little fingernail	Heart 9	Anger, Love
12.	Karate Chop Point (Outside edge of your hand)	Small Intestine 3	Sorrow – Joy

13. Energy Chord—Hold one finger on the "3rd eye" and one finger under the lip. Take 3 deep breaths while continuing to focus on the issue.

Note: If one of the treatment points feels more relaxing/effective, spend more time stimulating that point as there may be more energy "trapped" in that meridian.

Neurological Disorganization

The reason for starting with the "belly button" correction is to correct what kinesiologists refer to as "polarity switching"; a deeper disruption of energy circuits and energy flow.

IMPORTANT! IMPORTANT! IMPORTANT!

If the treatment (rubbing or tapping) of the acupressure points doesn't take you lower than a 3 or 4 on the 10-point scale, your anxiety or issue has "overloaded" the system, i.e., disrupted the "circuit breaker." Start with the belly button correction again and repeat the treatment protocol.

It is not necessary to do the belly button correction every time. Only do it if the rubbing or tapping does not take you down to a one.

Psychological Reversal

This is related to Tibetan Energy Theory and the "figure 8" energy flow of the body. Psychological Reversal results when there is a subconscious belief that one cannot overcome the problem, or if there are subconscious self-sabotage issues involved.

Begin the treatment after the "belly button" correction by rubbing the Neurolymphatic Reflex clockwise. (Another metaphor: think of this brief procedure as an "electrical reset button.") This realigns the polarities, thus allowing the meridians to "receive" the energy being rubbed or tapped into them.

Enjoy, and best wishes for your success!
Lee Pulos Ph.D., A.B.P.P.

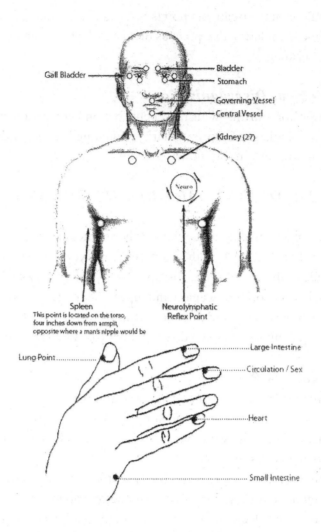

FOR MORE INFORMATION ON DR. LEE PULOS, EFT, HYPNOSIS AND VISUALIZATION TECHNIQUES PLEASE VISIT:

www.drpulos.com

Books—DVD's—CD Programs—MP3 Downloads—Seminars

Suggested Reading

1. *The Nature of Personal Reality* by Jane Roberts

2. *Higher Creativity* by Willis Harman, Ph.D.

3. *Psychocybernetics* by Dr. Maxwell Maltz

4. *Creative Visualization* by Shakti Gawain

5. *The Power of Now* by Eckhart Tolle

6. *Love is Letting Go of Fear* by Gerald Jampolsky, M.D.

7. *The Biology of Belief* by Bruce Lipton, Ph.D.

8. *The Inner Game of Tennis* by W. Timothy Gallwey

9. *The Brain That Changes Itself* by Norman Doidge, M.D.

10. *Seat of the Soul* by Gary Zukav

Acknowledgments

*My first acknowledgment is to **you**, the reader. The fact that the title of this book would be of interest to you speaks volumes of where you are in your own evolution. Thank you. I welcome you as a fellow change agent to assist in the transformation of the quality of life on our planet.*

Next, I would like to thank the more than 5,000 employees I have had the privilege to work with in three companies over a period of 30 years. Each company became the leading company within its respective industry. Many of the principles taught in this book were made widely available to our work force(s). For those who chose to drink the "Kool-Aid," I have witnessed many, many significant transformational changes both personally and professionally. "I love you (all) unconditionally."

To my life partner, Jeri, who has read the multiple drafts of my manuscript many times and provided her constructive input to help make this a better book.

And to my assistant of 17 years, Mary Fabish, who has typed every word in this book many, many times as well as her editorial contribution. Thank you so much Mary.

To our daughter, Julie, and son-in-law, Ted Kalmus, who surprised me on my 70th birthday and told me their present to me was four hours of reviewing the latest draft of my book. They had clandestinely procured a copy of my draft from Mary. Their observations and input led to many changes in the final draft of the book.

To daughter, Jill, and her husband, Jason Anderson, for their input as well as assistance in graphic design. To our sons Brian, JJ and his beautiful wife, Wendy, for their continuing support. Special kudos to JJ and Wendy for their technical assistance.

And to the people who made it possible for you to be reading this now. Thank you Bill Gladstone, for your leadership and to all of the people at Waterside Productions, Inc., You are a remarkable team.

My heartfelt thanks to my longtime friend, Dr. Lee Pulos, who so generously gave of his time and professional expertise in making relevant and insightful contributions to this book. Your friendship has enriched my life through many fun-filled and intriguing journeys of adventure and discovery.

And lastly a very special thank you to Marfa Marketing Group led by its two principals, Silas Reynolds and breAnne Reeves. Also much appreciation to their teammates, David Brudnicki, Joe Gustav, and Justin VanNatta who spent countless hours in the design and formatting of this book as well as the preparation of our web site, www.7keystounlock.com. Thank you for your vision, cover design and the runway you have created to help ensure the readership we believe this book deserves.Thank you all so much.

Jim

Special Recognition

I would like to recognize an organization that has special meaning to me. I invite you to explore how its teachings may be of value to you in your life as well.

Institute of Noetic Sciences

Our Vision

The Institute of Noetic Sciences serves an emerging movement of globally conscious citizens dedicated to manifesting our highest capacities. We believe that consciousness is essential to a paradigm shift that will lead to a more sustainable world. We encourage open-minded explorations of consciousness through the meeting of science and spirit. We take inspriation from the great discoveries of human history that have been sourced from insight and intuition and that have harnessed reason and logic for their outer expression. It is our conviction that systematic inquiries into consciousness will catalyze positive concrete transformations in the world. In this process, our vision is to help birth a new worldview that recognizes our basic interconnectedness and interdependence and promotes the flourishing of life in all its magnificent forms.

Our Mission

Broadening our knowledge of the nature and potentials of mind and consciousness and applying that knowledge to enhancing human well-being and the quality of life on the planet.

IONS has two locations
- EarthRise at IONS, our Retreat Center, is located on 200 acres of rolling hills about 10 minutes from downtown Petaluma.
101 San Antonio Rd., Petaluma, CA 94952 USA
- IONS' Research and Educational Offices are at Foundry Wharf on the Petaluma River in downtown Petaluma.
625 2nd St., Suite 200, Petaluma, CA 94952-5120
Tel: 707-775-3500
Fax: 707-781-7420
Web site: www.noetic.org

CPSIA information can be obtained at www.ICGtesting.com
Printed in the USA
LVOW03s0226300615

444383LV00016B/180/P